Three Comedies

Para Hilario y Jesús
de su compañero del alma
un afecto de siempre,
en la amistad

Raúl

For Hilario + Jesús —
with many good wishes —

Peter Holt

Three Comedies

Behind the Scenes in Eden

Rigmaroles

The Other William

by Jaime Salom

edited by Gregory J. Racz *and translated by* Marion Peter Holt, Gregory J. Racz, & Phyllis Zatlin

University Press of Colorado

Published by the University Press of Colorado
5589 Arapahoe Avenue, Suite 206C
Boulder, Colorado 80303

AAUP The University Press of Colorado is a proud member of
the Association of American University Presses.

The University Press of Colorado is a cooperative publishing enterprise supported, in part, by Adams State College, Colorado State University, Fort Lewis College, Mesa State College, Metropolitan State College of Denver, University of Colorado, University of Northern Colorado, and Western State College of Colorado.

The paper used in this publication meets the minimum requirements of the American National Standard for Information Sciences—Permanence of Paper for Printed Library Materials. ANSI Z39.48-1992

Library of Congress Cataloging-in-Publication Data

Salom, Jaime, 1925–
  [Dramas. English. Selections]
  Three comedies : Behind the scenes in Eden, Rigmaroles, and The other William / by Jaime Salom ; edited by Gregory J. Racz and translated by Marion Peter Holt, Gregory J. Racz, & Phyllis Zatlin.
    p. cm.
  Includes bibliographical references.
  ISBN 0-87081-780-9 (hardcover : alk. paper) — ISBN 0-87081-781-7 (pbk. : alk. paper)
  I. Racz, Gregory Joseph. II. Holt, Marion Peter. III. Zatlin, Phyllis, 1938– IV. Title.
  PQ6669.A55A24 2004
  862'.64—dc22

                                                                                    2004012147

Text design and typesetting by Laura Furney
Jacket design by Daniel Pratt

13   12   11   10   09   08   07   06   05   04   10   9   8   7   6   5   4   3   2   1

Cover photograph from Historias íntimas del paraíso *(Behind the Scenes in Eden)*

Support for this publication was generously provided by the Program for Cultural Cooperation between Spain's Ministry of Culture and United States Universities.

For Margarita Navarro Baldeweg

Contents

THREE COMEDIES

Introduction

Jaime Salom: A Life in Theater

For more than four decades, popular and critical acclaim has regularly accompanied the singular dramatic output of Jaime Salom. This retired ophthalmologist from Catalonia, an esteemed elder statesman of Madrid's theater world, has remained a steady countervailing force to the momentary tyranny of fleeting artistic vogues and continues to be one of Spain's most successful playwrights. Salom's sprawling oeuvre defies ready summary even as the confounding diversity of his forty-plus plays grows more complex with each new work produced. This remarkably varied collection repeatedly resists authoritative discussion of "typical" subject matters, "usual" modes of expression, or "characteristic" techniques. Over the course of his career, Salom has been the winner of the coveted National Literature Prize and was twice awarded the Espectador y la Crítica Prize for the best play of the year staged in Madrid. It is difficult not to marvel at the succession of prestigious theatrical honors his work has won: the Crítica de Barcelona (twice), Fraga, Bravo, Fastenrath, Álvarez Quintero, and Espinosa y Cortina Prizes, the last three awarded by the Spanish Royal Academy. Salom's artistic production has not been limited to dramatic genres; he is also the author of two novels, scores of essays, television scripts, and adaptations of both Max Frisch's *Die Chinesische Mauer* and Brendan Behan's *The Hostage*. Remarkably, given the trajectory of his distinguished career, it is still too early to speculate about Salom's permanent place in Spanish literary history, as the author, born in Barcelona on Christmas Day, 1925, remains as active a dramatist as ever. He has premiered, at the pace characteristic of his sustained productivity, five plays over the last seven years.

The far-reaching cultural tragedy of twentieth-century Spain remains the devastation unleashed on artistic production under the repressive Franco dictatorship (1939–1975) following the Spanish Civil War (1936–1939). Salom was not yet a teenager at the outbreak of what would be his nation's defining modern conflict, a vengeful, punishing war that, by some estimates, claimed the lives of a million Spaniards and would leave its bloody imprint on the country's psyche for decades. Within this historical context, Salom's dramatic activity predictably reflects the various shifts in intellectual climate vis-à-vis the flourishing of the arts and receptivity to new ideas. An early spate of rather conventional "morality plays" met no resistance from hard-line authorities. However, once Salom undertook to write plays of more immediate sociopolitical relevance at the waning of the Franco regime, he did encounter increased hostility from critics and some unwanted attention from official precincts. Censors predictably kept their eyes on Salom's developing interest in historical drama. Both the theatergoing public and the authorities noticed the growth in Salom's personal perspective on the nature of existence to accommodate the human desire for greater individual freedom and self-determination. In light of this evolution of tolerance and sympathy, the author came to be embraced not so much as the playwright of conscientious objection to autocratic rule as something less political and therefore more enduring. Today, Jaime Salom is best characterized as one of the leading dramatic figures to play out onstage the messy moral quandaries of what it means to lead a good life in Francoist and democratic Spain. Salom's reputation to date remains that of a dramatist not given to easy moral dicta, a writer profoundly engaged with the confusing philosophical intricacies of everyday existence.

Salom's achievements as one of Spain's foremost contemporary playwrights, flowering as they did at a critical moment in his nation's history, have garnered him his share of international renown. Besides the numerous stagings of his plays throughout the Spanish-speaking Americas, a number of Salom's works have been translated into French, Portuguese, Italian, German, Arabic, Romanian, Flemish, Slovak, and Catalan. Two of his plays, in fact—the early *sainete-*

like *La gran aventura* [The Big Adventure] (1961) and *La lluna de Valencia* [The Moon Over Valencia] (1992), a musical version of *El señor de las patrañas* (Rigmaroles) (1990)—were originally written in the language of his native Catalonia. Later in 1990 his play *Las Casas, una hoguera al amanecer* (Bonfire at Dawn) would be the first to premiere in Spanish abroad, in Mexico City—understandable given its subject matter. Salom's budding reputation outside Spain received an added boost with the publication in 1982 of Phyllis Zatlin's volume on the playwright in the Twayne's World Authors Series, a study that served as the writer's formal introduction to English-speaking audiences. Over the next decade, translations of Salom's works began to appear in English, and productions of his plays were staged intermittently in England and the United States. Salom's 1994 work, *Una noche con Clark Gable* [A Night With Clark Gable], was produced in Spanish at New York City's Thalia Theater. Since that time, Salom's works in translation have been available to English-language readers in a steady trickle. New York City's Puerto Rican Traveling Theater staged both Spanish and English productions of *Una hora sin televisión* (One Hour Without Television), *La playa vacía* (The Empty Beach), and *La piel del limón* (Bitter Lemon) in the late 1990s. It is hoped that the present volume, the first selection of Jaime Salom plays to be published in English, will contribute to his increasing international stature.

ETHICAL CONSERVATISM IN SALOM'S EARLY THEATER

Although Salom would not celebrate an actual staged performance of a play until *El mensaje* [The Message] premiered in Bilbao in 1955, his playwriting considerably predates this production. Salom was awarded the Teatro Español Universitario Prize in 1948 for *Mamá sonríe* [Mama Is Smiling], a play he had written the previous year, which, along with *Ha pasado una vida* [A Life Is Over] (1946), *La hora gris* [The Gray Hour] (1952), and the undatable *La noche en blanco* [The Sleepless Night], the author persists—perhaps unjustly—in considering unsophisticated juvenalia. Salom's gradual road to success over the next decade might be sketched briefly as follows: his 1960 play, *El triángulo blanco* [The White Triangle], was the first to be performed in Barcelona, and his next effort the same year, *Verde esmeralda* [Emerald Green], was staged in Spain's capital. Salom's subsequent detective drama *Culpables* [The Guilty] (1961) represents his first popular and critical hit, whereas the poetic fantasy *El baúl de los disfraces* [The Trunk of Disguises] (1964) is widely considered his first true work of original theater. A few moral melodramas intervened before *La casa de las*

El baúl de los disfraces (The Trunk of Disguises) (1964)

Chivas (The House of the Chivas) (1968) ran for 1,343 consecutive performances in Madrid, putting Salom on the map of twentieth-century Spanish theater. This groundbreaking treatment of a group of soldiers and civilians surviving near the front lines during the Spanish Civil War marked the end of a prevailing ethical conceptualization of theater to which Salom would never quite return.

The most transparent reason for Salom's critical self-distancing from many of his earliest dramatic efforts is their shared moral conservatism and preoccupation with guilt, responsibility, and familial duty. Raised in an observant Catholic household, the product of a Jesuit high school who came of age precisely as Spain fell under Franco's *nacionalcatolicismo* brand of fascism, Salom repudiated his unquestioning espousal of traditional Spanish values at about the time the twilight of the Franco dictatorship came into view. The end of the tumultuous 1960s, which saw the violent repression of student demonstrations in Barcelona, Franco's willful loosening of his authoritarian grip on the government, and Salom's growing discontent in his marriage with divorce still illegal in Spain, ushered in a nearly simultaneous change in the author's worldview—a general liberalization toward issues of social and political import with a more accepting stance toward the frailties and mysteries of the human condition. For critics accustomed to Salom's reliable reinforcement of the sanctity of marriage, individual subjugation to the church, and filial bonds of respect, this incremental shift toward a more relative and open dramatic treatment of psychological complexity seemed both perplexing and needlessly jarring. Reviewers sniped at an author they deemed a mere writer of entertaining comedies and crime dramas suddenly aspiring to the creation of serious literature. As might be expected, this sort of commentary was not devoid of political motivation. A brief synopsis of *Culpables,* a pop-genre murder mystery, will illustrate what Spanish theatergoers of the early 1960s might typically have expected from a Salom drama of the period.

Rogelio, a wealthy businessman, pays a surprise visit to the office of Dr. Andrés La Plaza, who is having an affair with his wife, Silvia. Instead of angrily confronting Andrés, Rogelio proposes that the doctor sign a false death certificate so Rogelio can avoid imprisonment for his bankrupt business by fleeing Spain and living off his life-insurance policy, thus leaving Silvia and Andrés free to marry. Battling his conscience, Andrés officially documents that Rogelio has succumbed to heart failure, and all goes well until a year later, when Inspector Ruiz shows up from Madrid. It seems anonymous letters have been arriving at police headquarters claiming Rogelio was in reality poisoned. Ruiz informs

Viaje en un trapecio (Trapeze Ride) (1970)

Silvia and Andrés, who are about to wed, that Rogelio's body, which they both know is not in the coffin, must be exhumed for tests. When a decomposed corpse is disinterred, Andrés begins to suspect Silvia of duplicity, even murder.

Although Ruiz assures the doctor that Silvia could not have killed Rogelio, a troubled Andrés confesses his lie and urges Ruiz to provide him with absolute assurance of his future wife's moral character. The inspector soon discovers that Rogelio's life insurance is being withdrawn from a Swiss bank by Salvador García, Rogelio's shady business partner. Andrés's former office assistant, secretly in love with the doctor for years, tries to clear him of suspicion by falsely admitting to having sent the letters herself. By this time, though, the astute Ruiz has solved the perplexing mystery: the body found in the coffin is actually that of García, whose embezzlement and attempted sexual blackmail of Silvia compelled Rogelio to strangle him. Rogelio is now living comfortably in Switzerland under his dead partner's identity, and it is learned that Rogelio himself has sent the letters, hoping to foment suspicion between the rigidly ethical Andrés and the unfaithful wife he still desires. At the play's close, Rogelio appears in Andrés's office armed with a pistol and asks Silvia to choose between the two men, knowing that the events he has set in motion will have diminished Silvia's love for someone who could harbor so much doubt about her conduct and personality. Silvia then kills Rogelio, but not before she poses the question of who the guilty parties in this tawdry episode of infidelity, fraud, duplicity, and murder truly are.

For audiences used to the light appeal of whodunit suspense and conventional morality, it is little wonder that Salom's subsequent dramatic works would cause such a stir.

POLITICAL ENGAGEMENT IN SALOM'S MATURE DRAMAS

By the mid-1960s Salom had put aside such conventional productions to move in more substantive and compelling dramatic directions. Beginning with *La casa de las Chivas* and proceeding through *Los delfines* [The Heirs Apparent] (1969), *La noche de los cien pájaros* [The Night of the Hundred Birds] (1972), and *La piel del limón* four years later, Salom settled into a second phase of more socially and politically aware theater that coincided with the demise of Franco's once fearsomely autocratic rule. *La casa de las Chivas* is a prime example of the daring Salom began to exhibit in the never innocent (or isolated) world of theater under dictatorship. The play not only sympathetically depicts soldiers and civilians in their daily reactions to the ever-present threat of death in wartime but represents the first staging of Spain's definitive twentieth-century conflict as seen through the eyes of the losing republican partisans. Such a perspective would have seemed inconceivable only a few decades earlier, as Franco's

La casa de las Chivas (The House of the Chivas) (1968)

deadly retaliation against those who had fought against his fascist forces contin-ued long after the war's end. *Los delfines,* too, portrayed in timely dramatic fashion the gradual dissolution of the once powerful Tuser family of industrialists in another oblique mirroring of an enfeebled and feckless regime. Following the death of the eighty-year-old patriarch Juan, his widow, Carolina, desper-ately connives to keep the business in family hands under the leadership of her son Fere. With ruthless single-mindedness of purpose, Carolina hopes to per-petuate total family control over the means of production, dismissing outright all talk of reforms such as power sharing with company employees. Progressive ideas coming from America, the New World's bastion of democracy, are held in contempt as transparent tricks to dispossess Tuser management of its economic stronghold, and Fere's antitraditionalist children want nothing to do with ill-gotten gains through capitalist oppression. *Los delfines* ends with Fere's suicide marking the inevitable dissolution of a once autonomous, isolationist system defiantly resistant to any form of change.

A few years later, *La noche de los cien pájaros* would similarly reflect the moral uncertainties surrounding an authoritarian regime in decline. The play depicts the relationship of Adrián and Juana, a couple married for two decades who, like Fere and his wife, Luisa, in *Los delfines,* have made their peace, acknowledg-ing that their happiest days are behind them. Sadly for the two, Adrián's latent discontent surfaces abruptly at the twentieth reunion of what would have been his law-school graduating class. Years back, he had dropped out and married beneath his social class when Juana's parents, who ran a meat stall, died suddenly and left her in desperate need of help with the family business. After beginning an affair with Lilián, a successful former classmate's secretary, Adrián plots to remove the sickly Juana from the picture by lacing her heart medicine with poison. Although Juana dies (ironically) without ensuring her husband's ex-pected happiness, Adrián is wracked not only by guilt but by plaguing doubt: Did Juana die a natural death, or was he actually successful in murdering her? Worse still, did Juana, aware of Adrián's lack of love for her, intentionally sacri-fice her life so her husband could find the happiness that eludes him at the play's end? In a clear departure from the catholic clarity of his earliest plays, *La noche de los cien pájaros* declines to impose ethical imperatives on its characters, sug-gesting that notions of right and wrong are perhaps inextricably bound up in the instantial moral quagmire that is everyday life.

The family as societal microcosm remained under siege in Salom's first play to premiere after Franco's death, *La piel del limón,* whose very title is a reminder

Los delfines (The Heirs Apparent) (1969)

of the perceived compulsion to keep up appearances in the face of inner turmoil and decay. The work is Salom's strongest argument for the place of divorce in civil society, a cause the playwright championed rigorously during Spain's halting return to constitutional monarchy. Juan and Rosa's emotionally dead marriage is held together primarily by consideration for their thirteen-year-old daughter, Alejandra, until Juan mistakenly believes he can find happiness outside the bonds of matrimony by living with his secretary, Bárbara, with whom he has long carried on an affair. In time, Juan is dispassionately reminded by his partner (and Rosa's cousin), Narciso, of the need to maintain outward propriety whatever the psychological cost, as his prolonged absence from home has begun to hurt their business. Intensifying this psychic conflict at the heart of the play is Salom's notorious decision to have Juan's daughter and lover be portrayed by the same actress in differing temporal planes. Juan has made up his mind to give his marriage another chance as the final scene opens with his return home for Alejandra's sixteenth birthday party, exactly three years after the action at the play's start. Bárbara's possible suicide is alluded to as *La piel del limón* ends with Juan and Rosa unable to resume conjugal relations in an atmosphere of frustrated self-determination reminiscent of the world outside the theater where rigid moral strictures once took absolute precedence over the reasoned alternative of personal choice.

Two political allegories produced ten years apart similarly bear witness to Salom's sustained engagement with the transformational history of his day. *Tiempo de espadas* (Time of Swords) (1972) is a radical retelling of the apostles' relationship to Jesus Christ, set in an unnamed country in the present. The play's imaginative recoding of Spain's political landscape at the end of the Franco dictatorship is, however, everywhere in evidence. The twelve followers of a recently sentenced revolutionary gather clandestinely in a restaurant's banquet room to discuss the future of their mission. Fearing arrest and uncertain of who should assume the group's leadership, the twelve demonstrate not only great personal differences but ideological dissent and even a possible misunderstanding of their captured leader's idea of deliverance. The pseudo-biblical aura surrounding the action of *Tiempo de espadas* underscores the totalitarian nature of the military regime parading triumphantly not only beneath the supper-club windows but, in a very real sense, outside the theater as well.

This pervasive aura of widespread, if impotent, political opposition is treated with comparable vagueness in *Un hombre en la puerta* [A Man at the Door] (1984), in which Víctor, the protagonist with notably liberal (even socialistic) tendencies, is expelled from a nondescript group of delegates. Fearing for his life like the disciple figures of *Tiempo de espadas,* he takes temporary refuge in the home of his ex-lover Miriam, who now lives with her lesbian partner, Berta. As

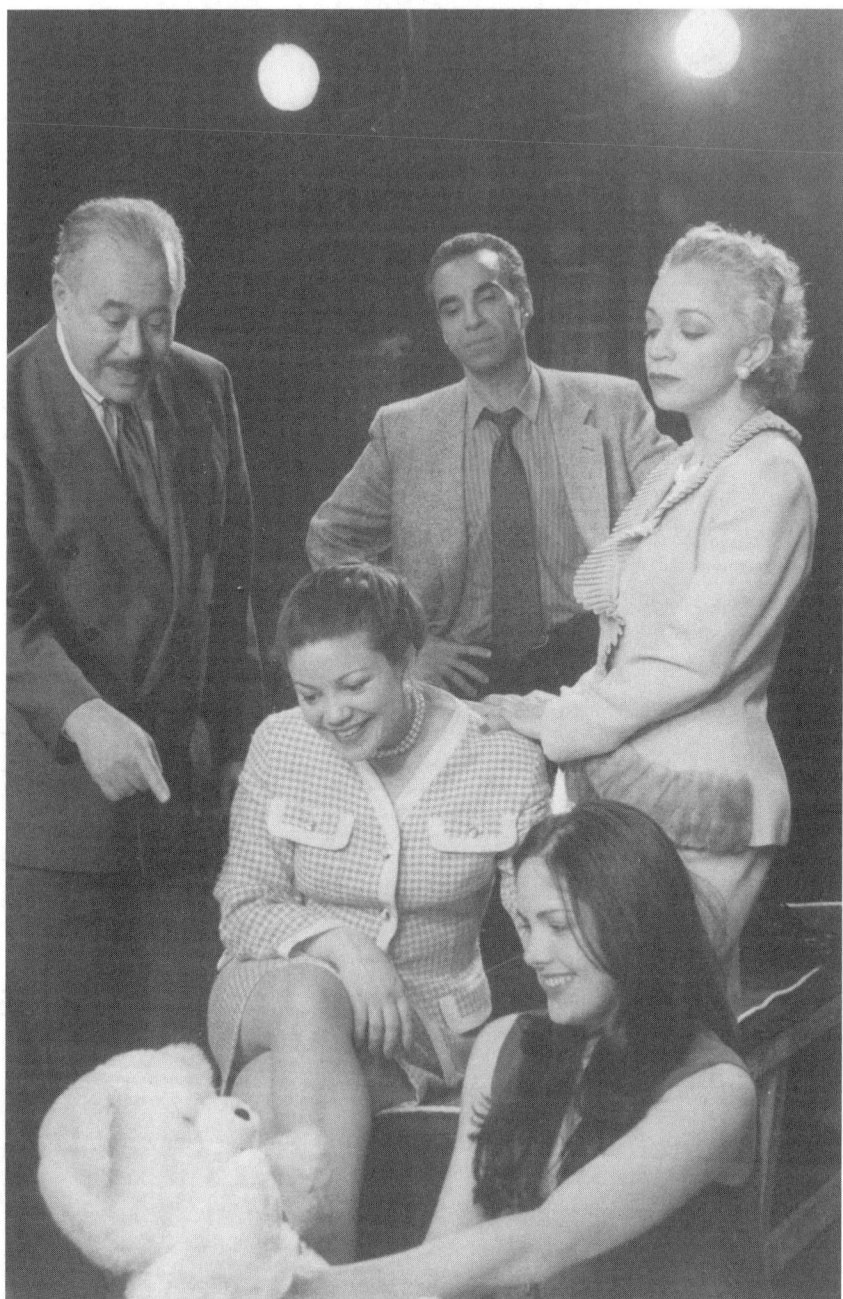

La piel del limón (Bitter Lemon)

Tiempo de espadas (Time of Swords) (1972)

in the play's earlier counterpart, no precise reference is ever made to a political leader, although *El hombre en la puerta* does contain language directly stating the need for a democratizing youth movement to replace the autocratic decision making of some head of state for life. The work thus plays out the complications of the characters' sexual triangle against a political backdrop pessimistic about the possibility of systemic change from within and with a phantom presence typical of the works of this phase. Not surprisingly, Salom, one of Spain's principal advocates for a return to normalcy after decades of reactionary politics, declared the tense and poignant *Tiempo de espadas* to be his favorite work of the twenty-plus he had written at that point in his career.

GROWTH OF A FEMINIST SENSIBILITY

After this politically charged period of provocative output, Salom's plays have increasingly showcased a wide range of subjects and a variety of innovative stage techniques. Not since early in his career has Salom premiered plays back-to-back dealing with a similar topic or pertaining to the same dramatic category, and his oeuvre of the 1980s and 1990s is, in comparison, strikingly eclectic. The sheer scope of these more recent dramas has allowed Salom, in step with his liberal shift on social issues, to focus on the imaginative reworking of themes with which he has also since become identified, including the resonance of history in contemporary life, the driving need for freedom of being and expression, and the "equality" (often suggested through parallelism or doubling) between upper and lower classes, authors and actors or their characters, and men and women. Especially notable among these is Salom's focus on the role of women in Spanish society. Following the broad comic portrayal of the Walter Mittyish Leoncia in *Cita los sábados* [Saturday Night Date] (1967) as a bored provincial housewife living out a series of fanciful adventures during a weekly game of Parcheesi, Salom's female characters have increasingly acquired the multidimensionality and psychological realism they often lacked in his earlier works. Salom's change in worldview is reflected in his concerted efforts to develop these characters sympathetically and give voice to their protests against the subtle (and not so subtle) ways in which they remain oppressed by Spanish society at large. Indeed, some of Salom's most recent works have featured starring female roles written specifically with leading Spanish actresses in mind.

Even before his creation of Juana's domestic tragedy in *La noche de los cien pájaros,* Salom explored the unique solitude women face in *La playa vacía,* indisputably his most metaphorical and metaphysical play to date. These qualities have led some to view the work, produced after *Los delfines* during what is still Salom's most important and innovative period, as a kind of modern-day, profane *auto sacramental.* The widowed Victoria, facing a long, lonely off-season following the death of an elderly companion at the seaside resort she runs, implores Pablo, a beachcombing hired hand, to keep her company during the winter. Although Victoria, who is of a certain age, assures Pablo she is not paying him for sexual services, the two soon become involved until the younger Tana, a mysterious presence literally from beyond the waves, washes up seemingly lifeless onshore. Her appearance complicates Victoria's neat plans for time with Pablo, as do the sporadic visits of her affable older supplier, the kindly, paternalistic, and somehow otherworldly Don. Although it is evident that each character symbolizes a potent existentialist force (Life, Sexual Pleasure, Death, and God, respectively), Salom manages to limn the bleakness of Victoria's situation realistically enough for viewers to despair at her decision to drown herself by play's end. Still, because of *La playa vacía*'s obvious symbolic veneer and experimentation with ontological themes, Victoria ultimately lacks full devel-

Una hora sin televisión (One Hour Without Television)

opment as a flesh-and-blood female character, however reminiscent her circumstances of the hopeless entrapment Salom came to see as typical of a woman's position in Spain.

This feminist sensibility has become a hallmark of Salom's mature works and is almost invariably on display in his more recent plays. Salom's sobering social commentary on Spanish machismo, *Una hora sin televisión,* provides a fine example of the difficulties even successful and seemingly independent wives face in confronting their husbands' general peccadilloes and inattentiveness. In this rare two-character drama, Patricia is reduced to begging the philandering Eduardo for the titular hour without television as the anniversary gift he has predictably forgotten to buy her. The play unfolds in real time as the sports-loving, model-seducing Eduardo finally threatens to shoot Patricia if she leaves him for the sensitive musical impresario she has elaborately described to him. Thoroughly unaware of this relationship, Eduardo is unable to tease Patricia for her impressive choice of a lover, so unlike the mousy violinist who had previously won her affections. After eighteen years of belittling her talents and ambitions as a pianist, Eduardo experiences his own emotional abandonment when

Patricia decides to leave her predicament, only to face the uncertainties that follow a woman after a broken marriage. Patricia's hopeful resolve to walk out on her husband in favor of a life of increased freedom and independence falters at play's end, providing an apt commentary on the limits to female liberty outside of marriage that Salom's dramas repeatedly decry. Although *Una hora sin televisión* ultimately leaves open the possibility that Patricia will reconsider her hasty return home, she is left suffering the miseries of near-total estrangement as the curtain falls.

There may be no better measure of the evolution in Salom's conceptualization and handling of female characters than his treatment of the relationships between two pairs of sisters, created over thirty years apart, in *Espejo para dos mujeres* [A Mirror for Two Women] (1965) and *Más o menos amigas* [Friends More or Less] (1999). Both plays present mismatched siblings, a homecoming, an emotional rapprochement, and a final decision concerning cohabitation. Although neither set of sisters can be considered the fully individualized ideal of psychological realism that has become the standard in mimetic dramatization, Salom's approach to these characters nevertheless illustrates the shift in social outlook and artistic temperament representative of the trajectory of his long career. In *Espejo para dos mujeres,* essentially a Christian morality play, Tina returns home to live with her younger sister, Laura, in northern Spain following the death of her atheist French husband many years after their disapproving father has passed away. Laura, who was left to care for the family (and who still looks after their dying maid, Patricia), is a model of self-sacrifice and charity in welcoming Tina back, oblivious to both her sister's philandering and their father's sexual hypocrisy. Laura's discovery that Patricia's apparently groundless hatred of her stems from a past encounter in which their outwardly respectable father insisted that the maid abort their illegitimate child happens after she learns that Tina has returned home with her lover, Peter, in tow. The play ends with the slightly cardboard figures of the sisters—one the paragon of virtue, the other the too worldly libertine—deciding to stay together in Spain despite their mutual love for Peter, who has expressed his own love privately for the virginal Laura. The sisters embrace melodramatically at play's close, affirming their filial duty to each other above romantic involvement with an attractive, reformed bon vivant left stranded at the airport, phoning frantically.

In contrast to the stock-character quality of Tina and Laura, Flora and Dora in *Más o menos amigas* are so fluidly, comically, and outrageously delineated that it might be said Salom chose to sacrifice fidelity to real-life characterization in favor of the suggestive veracity of ironic excess. Flora, a slightly fastidious homebody, has gone to live with her foul-mouthed sister, Dora, a dubiously talented nightclub singer, after their mother's death. Dora's slovenliness grates reciprocally on Flora, who sets the action in motion by dating a would-be impresario who mistakes her at first for Dora, then shows up only sporadically to see her. Dora, too, is plagued by an apparently unfaithful suitor, her accompanist, Pipper; and after Flora and Dora find improbable success singing as a duo, the two set out to put their love lives in order. Dora's harsh dismissal of Flora's Fernando leads Flora to send Pipper packing, until it is learned in a brisk comic coda that both pairs have remained together as couples. Unlike the very different sisters in *Espejo para dos mujeres,* at the end of *Más o menos amigas* Flora and Dora opt not to live with each other, as Dora is appalled by her sister's chubby twins and bourgeois lifestyle while Flora laments her sister's increasingly risqué cabaret act. In comparison with the dated sentimentalism of Laura and Tina in *Espejo para dos mujeres,* the sisters in *Más o menos amigas* are drawn with such unrestrained gusto that they appear to embody, however comically, the infinite possibilities of individual growth and potential. Despite their humorous shortcomings, Flora and Dora exude the dramatic vitality of two female characters with irremediable limitations, yet unstintingly and vivaciously alive.

SALOM'S DRAMATIZATION OF SPANISH HISTORY

A runaway hit that secured its author's place among the major modern dramatists of Spain, *La casa de las Chivas* was Salom's first play to deal unequivocally with a historical subject. Although it might be argued that earlier works of primarily bourgeois sensibility—domestic dramas and light comedies concerning the interaction of family members or couples—were at least imbued with the restrictive ethos of Franco's Spain, *La casa de las Chivas* broke the mold, inaugurating a succession of variously serious, comic, sometimes farcical plays whose sustained focus was Spanish history as seen anachronistically through the prism of dictatorship. Whereas Salom may be most revered and best remembered for this cluster of plays produced between 1968 and 1976, a sufficient amount of his work from 1978 to the present explores historical themes to have tempted critics to consider these a kind of collective sociopolitical docudrama. Indeed, the three plays composing this volume are comedic variants of the extremely serious looks at history effected in the works discussed here from the same period.

El corto vuelo del gallo (The Cock's Short Flight) (1980)

El corto vuelo del gallo (The Cock's Short Flight) (1980), the first Spanish play ever to depict Franco as a "character" onstage—an empty chair at the reading of his mother's will—was predictably greeted with vociferous protests from the lingering fascist faithful. As in the foreboding works of shadowy political intrigue mentioned earlier and even in *La casa de las Chivas,* Franco is ever present, more notably here through his conspicuous physical absence. His menacing presence hovers palpably over the action of the entire play, whose central figure is Franco's father, Nicolás, a foul-mouthed, ill-tempered, skirt-chasing, generally dissolute republican with nothing but open contempt for his God-fearing, reactionary mama's boy of a son. Nicolás clearly favors his dashing aviator son, Ramón, who, it is implied, was shot down by Spanish planes once his own antifascist sympathies began to garner embarrassing attention. The play is remarkable for its cold-eyed treatment of the effects of childhood emotional trauma on the male psyche and is openly provocative in its intimations regarding the psychological formation of a totalitarian. Besides having the same actor play many of the bit functionary roles and one actress portray both Nicolás's daughter Pilar (by his pious wife of the same name) and Agustina, the child of the long-suffering woman with whom he lives, the play employs a fluid temporal plane in which the dead Pilar (Franco's mother) and Ramón occasionally

Las Casas, una hoguera al amanecer (Bonfire at Dawn)

return to dialogue with Nicolás. In breaking an unspoken taboo concerning what could and could not be done with the memory of Franco, *El corto vuelo del gallo* helped usher in a more open phase of theater in democratic Spain.

The uncompromising nature of Salom's take on Spanish history and his courageous willingness to invite controversy are equally evident in *Las Casas, una hoguera al amanecer,* a dramatization of the life of the priest called the "Apostle of the Indies." Las Casas's brave efforts to counter the inhumane treatment of indigenous populations during the brutal Spanish conquest earned him enemies at court, among his Dominican superiors, and even among members of his family. Salom's Las Casas, in keeping with the author's keen grasp of human complexity, is no one-dimensional saint. Gently mocked for his interest in the priesthood after a youth filled with its share of dalliance, Las Casas is tinged with reckless idealism, stubborn intransigence, even self-serving hubris. His personality as delineated by the playwright's empathic vision is also nuanced by a certain moral cowardice—for example, does Las Casas send away his former Indian servant, Señor, to face death from exhaustion at the mines because he fears his own human frailty will lead him to reciprocate Señor's homosexual desire for him? Salom's harsh look at the events of the so-called Black Legend prevents both oppressor and oppressed from seeming unproblematically heroic. Bloody massacres resulting from indigenous uprisings, counterposed with the marauding savagery of unadulterated Spanish greed, ensure that neither conqueror nor conquered appears noble in the end.

In a pair of works approaching tragicomedy, Salom takes on two *monstres sacrés* of twentieth-century painting, Salvador Dalí and Pablo Picasso, exploring the psychic burden of Spanish creativity in a cosmopolitan setting. *Casi una diosa* (Almost a Goddess) (1993) takes its title from Dalí's worshipful treatment of his mistress and muse, Elena Diakonova (Gala), by turns fortune hunter, Circe figure, Christian mystic, slave driver, and paragon of artistic inspiration. What begins for the couple as a promising sexual triangle with Elena's first husband, French surrealist poet Paul Éluard, devolves into an unhappy union in which Elena, through sheer force of will, practically imprisons the irrepressibly free-spirited Dalí in their remote castle home. There, Dalí is compelled to produce ever more paintings for profit, however adulterated the art, while Elena openly pursues erotic encounters entertaining younger men. *Casi una diosa* treats wistfully the inevitable parting of Elena and Éluard, ill suited for each other in disposition and woefully mismatched in ambition, in stark contrast to the lunatic frenzy the play invokes surrounding the odd and mutually destructive relationship of Elena and Dalí. As in *El corto vuelo del gallo*, Salom makes poignant use of Éluard's continued presence beyond the grave and of an efficient multipurpose Other, who assumes whatever role the plot requires at the time. Compared with Dalí and his effete sensationalism, Elena emerges in a reversal of traditional gender roles as the true sacred monster exploiting the innocent talent and perverse affections of a feckless male *ingénu*.

The young Picasso, replete with impetuous artistic temperament, is portrayed in Salom's *Las señoritas de Aviñón* [The Demoiselles of Avignon] (2001) as the destabilizing element in a Barcelona brothel whose prostitutes he immortalizes in the famed portrait of the title. Insistent, penurious, with an overblown sense of his own potential, Picasso quickly makes a nuisance of himself to Madame Hortensia, who is preoccupied with the more pressing business of weathering her employees' simmering discontent. *Las señoritas de Aviñón* is less a play "about" Picasso than a colorful vignette of Catalonia at the turn of the twentieth century. The work focuses primarily on the interaction of the bordello's residents—the lesbians Antonia and Pepita; Picasso's favorite, Rosita; the depressive, man-hating Pilar; and Madame Hortensia's daughter, Sofía, who by play's end has succumbed to the life. Picasso's *succès de scandale* is revealed to the

Las señoritas de Aviñón (The Demoiselles of Avignon) (2001)

shock of the women, who understandably have difficulty recognizing themselves in his canvas. As they view their portraits displayed in a 1908 French
magazine, Picasso's painting is grandly projected on a screen at the rear of the
stage. Meanwhile, bombs exploding in the street and news of international
turmoil serve as a muted backdrop to the eleven short scenes that provide a lurid
but jaunty depiction of a bygone era. For some time Salom has been toying
with the idea of writing a third "Spanish painter" play about Joan Miró but has
quipped that Miró led too saintly a life to be the stuff of compelling drama—
except, perhaps, for Holy Week celebrations!

Two obviously farcical treatments of medieval history provide an apt contrast to the sometimes somber, sometimes seriocomic visions of the preceding
works. *Nueve brindis por un rey* [Nine Toasts for a King] (1974), notable for its
ironic tone and ludicrous anachronisms, contains at its core the tragic cause of
Catalonian marginalization in Spanish politics dating from the 1412 Compro-
mise of Caspe. The play sends up the failure to elect Louis of Anjou to succeed
the heirless King Martin I, making light of the church's rigidity and of bedrock
democratic principles, as in the scene in which delegates hold up placards U.S.
convention style in favor of their preferred candidates for sovereign. Through its

depiction of all the impossible back-room wrangling to enthrone Ferdinand I as king of Spain—a decision more a function of papal schisms and individual self-promotion than of communitarian considerations for the nation's best interests—the play never loses sight of this beginning of political irrelevancy for a fiercely independent province. In the work's encyclopedic coda, all the delegates at Caspe relate the mostly illustrious futures their compromised vote has garnered them, except Guillermo de Vallseca, Louis of Anjou's advocate, who is absent presumably for supporting the sole candidate who would have ensured Catalonian ascendancy. The implication, of course, is that this once prominent political figure is now not even a footnote to history.

Similarly, a planned rock opera, *Jerusalén, hora cero* [Jerusalem, Zero Hour], which Salom finished in 1995 after more than a decade of revision, is yet to be staged. The action, complete with musical score, provides a sardonic glance at the punctured idealism of a group of child crusaders during the Middle Ages who plan to set sail from Marseilles on a mission to bring peace and love to Muslim infidels. An odd departure from an already wide-ranging life's work, *Jerusalén, hora cero* is a rare bird in the Salom canon. As a play nonetheless very much engaged with the silly vagaries of history, it serves as a fitting transition to the works that compose the present collection.

THREE "HISTORICAL" COMEDIES FROM DEMOCRATIC SPAIN

Franco's death in 1975 after thirty-six years of dictatorship hastened the establishment of constitutional monarchy in Spain with the institution of parliamentary democracy and the restoration of the Borbón dynasty. For Salom, many of whose earlier works protested the right-wing repressions of their time, the promise of a freer, more open society facilitated the pursuit of new dramatic directions first explored in *Nueve brindis por un rey*. For the first time in his long career, Salom began to treat broadly historical subjects as occasions for humor, mockery, and send-up. Not since the early 1960s had Salom's dramatic output included such a large number of plays so comically ironic and lighthearted in tone. Alongside works conveying his continued interest in the psychology of contemporary relationships, Salom authored a series of comedies set, at least on the surface, ever farther from the often somber realities of twentieth-century Spain. The 1978 production of *Historias íntimas del paraíso* (Behind the Scenes in Eden) marks the start of an approximately twenty-five-year period encompassing the premieres of *El señor de las patrañas* (1990); its musical version in Catalan, *La lluna de Valencia* (1992); and *El otro William* (The Other William) (1998). Also during this time, Salom wrote the abovementioned *Jerusalén, hora cero* (published in 1995), *Aquel pícaro Madrid* [That Rascally Madrid], an homage to the nineteenth-century *costumbrista* Ramón de Mesonero Romanos (published in 1999), and *Esta noche no hay cine* [No Movies Tonight], which features a hapless production of *Othello* by a traveling theater troupe forced to use substitute actors (published in 2002 under the title *Este domingo no hay cine*). Collectively, these works represent a more recent phase of Salom's writing for the stage in which the imperative to respond artistically to political crisis yields to the (relative) luxury of unconstrained imaginative creation.

Salom's foray into "historical" comedy after his medieval farce *Nueve brindis por un rey* continued with a return to the dawn of creation in *Historias íntimas del paraíso*. Although it would be difficult to conceive of a setting more removed in time than the Garden of Eden, the play's antediluvian remoteness does not entirely divest its action of echoes of life under Spanish dictatorship. Nor do *El señor de las patrañas,* set in Renaissance Valencia, and *El otro William,* set in Elizabethan/Stuart England, rid their plots completely of connections to twentieth-century Spain. In contrast to his politically engaged works of the late 1960s and early 1970s, the three plays in this volume (and the others listed earlier) consistently remind viewers that history operates according to a kind of periodic, even circular chronology. The works endorse the old adage about history repeating itself as Salom, in choosing to dramatize symbolically charged eras, suggests a metaphorical quality to modes of existence outside a conventional movement of Time. Episodes and situations deemed unique to specific cultures or confined to certain generations are portrayed instead as palimpsests that reveal simultaneously past and present manifestations.

Thus, *Historias íntimas del paraíso* blurs strict temporal movement through a steady interjection of anachronism and hints at the interchangeability of individuals over time through Adam's replacement of his "wife," Lili, with Eve. The play relies on the religious resonance of Eden and the well-known biblical narrative of creation to unsettle viewers by demonstrating just how easily apparently objective "historical" record can be rewritten to serve political ends. In a similar vein, *El señor de las patrañas* makes exemplary use of dramatic irony by implicitly comparing the political intrigue of one dire moment in sixteenth-century Valencia with the memory of a not-too-distant Spanish past. The work's collapsing of linear time is continuously reinforced by the rigid symmetry of its two acts, in which overlapping rehearsals of the play within the play, parallel visits from a court emissary, and the explicit pairing of the roles of two young women imply the sustainable repetition of people, places, and events. *El otro William* likewise defies traditional chronology by literally beginning in a present that opens onto the past and employing a protagonist whose two roles straddle these divergent temporal planes. The work's very title signals the central doubling that drives the plot and argues once again for a plausible view of historical character and incident as more archetype and imbrication than novelty and particularity. One can scarcely imagine Salom indulging such an aesthetic conceptualization of history while writing plays directed against the policies and ethos of the Franco regime. Circular time would have provided little help for arguments levied against a government most Spanish artists and intellectuals considered a historical aberration and a peculiar blight to be permanently expunged.

Historias íntimas del paraíso—Behind the Scenes in Eden

Behind the Scenes in Eden is a comic retelling of the Judeo-Christian creation myth as it appears, somewhat contradictorily, in chapters 1 and 2 of *Genesis*. In the first version of the story, God creates Adam and Eve from the same clay, implying that the spouses are social equals. In the second, Eve is formed from Adam's rib and thus arguably is fashioned in man's image, not God's, in a subsequent stage. The play throughout is concerned with language, writing, authority, and books in general; its subplot involves the effacing of Lilith, Adam's purported first wife alluded to in nonbiblical Jewish texts, from "official" biblical sources. The imaginative premise of *Behind the Scenes in Eden* proposes that the two creation narratives actually refer to separate acts, from which Lilith sprang first and Eve only after Adam had tired of her predecessor's resolute insistence on equality. Before the expulsion from paradise that closes the play, Adam ensures that the "Lord's Diary" or "official record book" makes no mention of Lili (as she is named here), replacing her role in prompting the first couple's flight from Eden with the improbable substitution of a talking serpent.

Behind the Scenes in Eden makes excellent use of a mere four characters, the Adam-Lili-Eve triangle being joined by Angel, an alternately haughty and career-minded functionary just promoted to the new post in paradise. The play thus treats God as a sort of invisible CEO, introduced by Angel in the opening lines as He is being helicoptered away for His Sabbath/weekend rest. Determined not to return to the uninspiring bureaucratic departments from which he has been transferred, Angel assumes more than a rooting interest in the smooth development of the relationship between Adam and Lili, who are ill suited for

Historias íntimas del paraíso (Behind the Scenes in Eden)

each other from the start. The consummate protofeminist, Lili demands equal consideration for her status as a woman, as Adam takes every opportunity to insist (sometimes violently) on his authority, superiority, and primacy. At times, in fact, Adam appears to be the only truly discordant element in the heaven-on-earth in which he has been placed, so it is hardly challenging for contemporary theatergoers to cast blame for the events in Eden where it really belongs.

At the play's premiere, Salom was dismayed by Spanish audiences' visceral negative reaction to the sympathetic character of Lili, whose uncompromising stance toward women's rights they considered strident, upsetting, even revolutionary at the time. Perhaps it should come as no surprise that Salom's advocacy of gender equality would face the sort of opposition it did in the early years of Spain's return to constitutional democracy. Viewers' widespread siding with the dull, doll-like Eve over the progressive and self-determined Lili may well be taken as a sad measure of just how reflexive and ingrained Spanish conservatism had become. Given the repressive air surrounding social and sexual mores on and off stage, it comes as little surprise that Act One ends with an expected separation, whereas Act Two bears speedy witness to adultery.

As glib as the play is in its tone and treatment of what feminist scholars have called "phallogocentrism," *Behind the Scenes in Eden* manages to raise almost every serious question related to women's struggle for equal rights. Whereas many of Salom's plays bear highly personalized dedications, *Behind the Scenes in Eden* is preceded by these words in the Spanish edition: "For the many Liliths who defend the dignity of women in this our unjust society" (translation mine). Indeed, before she exits from the stage of paradise, Lili addresses—however obliquely—the issues of birth control and family planning, child care, the pursuit of sexual pleasure, freedom of choice, respect for personal opinion, participation in decision making, and self-determination. Lili, from her first appearance onstage, protests the failure to consider her preferences for a desirable mate. Adam consistently declines to take Lili's remonstrations seriously despite his obvious physical attraction to her and his subsequent yearning for her intellectual prowess. Lili's innate understanding of the dire consequences of inequality within marriage assumes a prophetic guise by the close of Act One, as her words to Adam prove to be ominously on the mark: "This invention of man and woman can work marvelously well, you know, but it's so carefully equilibrated that when one of them tugs the cord too hard, the whole thing can be wrecked in a moment."

Salom's decision to clothe Adam and Lili in the same casual attire of a T-shirt and faded jeans underscores the relaxed edenic environment soon to be destroyed while providing an apt contrast to both the silly "feminine" frilliness of Eve and the literally sexless starchiness of Angel. Adam's oppositional machismo notwithstanding, his male member is declared an ugly protuberance in the scene in which Lili, he, and Angel display their physical sexual differences to one another. As Adam and his two extremely distinct helpmates play out the debate of what proper gender roles should be, Angel's epicene being and occasional exasperated huffiness emphasize Adam's brutal masculinity in its various guises: forbidding Lili to eat apples, insisting on sexual relations in the missionary position, destroying books he deems dangerous or incomprehensible, suggesting that women would be better treated if they yielded to man's idealizing will, and breaking the (phallic) flute Lili has carved in perceived competition with Adam's inferior instrument making. As Angel at times speaks lines that may be perceived as masturbatory (as an ethereal being he is sufficient unto himself) or even homosexual (he bristles whenever Adam urges him to imagine the

Historias íntimas del paraíso (Behind the Scenes in Eden)

latter's sexual relations with women), his character permits ample acting and directorial leeway to be maximized as the comic foil he embodies.

In the end, the excision of Lili from what is, in essence, the record of the world returns the play's focus to male authorial control over writing. A central irony of *Behind the Scenes in Eden* is that Adam, who ultimately pens the revisionist history of Eden, finds books heavy going and reading boring, whereas Lili laps up all the knowledge texts contain. Salom has great fun introducing anachronisms into Eden, a place where words, and not merely the abstract concepts they signify, were themselves new. Thus, the mention of "bubble bath," "kitchen," and "X-rays," to name a few, heightens the pathos in the coining of another series of far more meaningful utterances that practically chart the doomed course of human creation: "paradise," "man," "tree," "wife," "apple," "love," "kiss," "copulate," "reconciliation," "nostalgia," "longing," "sadness," and "civilization." Adam's distaste for proscriptive norms leads him to shred divinely authored texts such as *Planning for the Human Family, Practical Guide for Sexual Justice, Women's Rights,* and *Male-Female Equality,* substituting his own discriminatory precepts for what is generally deemed to be God's benign rule. In the end, perhaps, Lili's objection to "a marriage like this, by royal edict," may serve as a blanket condemnation of all male hierarchical structures. Whether such a unilaterally oppressive system is imposed by God, Adam, or, in Spain's particular case, Franco, theatergoers may well agree with Lili's assessment (in the play's first version) of a reality in which one finds oneself without a voice: "This is a dictatorship!"

EL SEÑOR DE LAS PATRAÑAS—RIGMAROLES

Rigmaroles is based loosely on events in the life of the Valencian tanner, printer, and author Juan Timoneda (1520?–1583), whose importance to literature is better measured by his publication of early Spanish Golden Age writers (such as Seville playwright Lope de Rueda) than by the centrality of his own poetry, drama, and narrative. At best a minor Renaissance figure, Timoneda is today most commonly remembered for *El Patrañuelo* (1567), a popular collection of twenty-two mostly risqué narrative shorts known as *patrañas,* a genre translatable by dictionary definition as "tall tales," "yarns," "cock-and-bull stories," or the word that supplies the English-language title of the play. *Rigmaroles* places the salty sexual content of Timoneda's writing front and center in its opening lines, the coda of a bawdy play Juan has just composed for Valencia's upcoming festival. That these comic verses scandalize Juan's faux-proper wife, Isabel, to the point where she douses her husband with water underscores just how inappropriate they should be, but tellingly are not, for the Catholic celebration they were written to honor. The tension between the religious and secular realms in Valencian society is thus put on display from the very start and provides the philosophical backdrop to the action. As might be expected of any Salom historical comedy, this "Renaissance" farce and costume drama is also imbued with echoes of similarly dispiriting twentieth-century events.

Acts One and Two of *Rigmaroles* frame the play within the play that is the ongoing rehearsal of Juan's festival drama, which features a promisingly salacious cast of characters: cuckolded royal cousins, a humpbacked court jester, an innkeeper's daughter, and a traveling puppeteer. Around these parallel stagings the play's two simultaneous plot lines unfold, inextricably intertwined with questions of money, sex, and power: the growing fortune and influence of the Timoneda family, and the prospective happiness in love and marriage of Isabel's orphaned niece, Anna. Signs of a felicitous outcome to both initially seem propitious with the arrival at the solidly middle-class Timoneda residence of the Secretary to the Court, an aging widower who appears at first to be asking for the comely

El señor de las patrañas (Rigmaroles)

Anna's hand in marriage. The union would, of course, be a fabulous social match for this dispossessed young woman of dubious modesty, who is sexually involved not only with her cousins Vincent and Batista but with her uncle Juan. As the lecherous Secretary is the confidant at court to the libidinous Vicereine, facilitating the match proffers great promise for Juan's printing business and imminent membership in the Brotherhood of the Holy Blood, formerly reserved for men of noble birth. The Secretary's intention to live with Anna in concubinage, however, coupled with the Vicereine's sudden downturn in health, frustrates both possibilities, as a somberly attired Secretary reappears in Act Two forecasting the intellectual repressions of the coming Counter Reformation. The denouement of *Rigmaroles* concerns the aggrieved Timoneda family's response to the erratic Lord Patriarch's censoring of Juan's writing and to the Secretary's order that the rejected Anna live out her days in a convent.

Prostitution—not only of the body but of one's talents, morals, and ideals—may well be the overarching theme of *Rigmaroles* and is nowhere more evident than in the implicit comparison between Anna and Purity, the ironically named prostitute who replaces Juan's niece in the rehearsals of the play within the play. Anna, for whom Juan and Isabel hope to make an advantageous marriage, is far more immodest than the faithful and (improbably for her profession) virginal Purity, who spends her days pining for her Aniceto to return from seeking his fortune in the New World. Thus, whereas Anna lustily applauds the raucous action of Juan's play, Purity expresses her scruples at its immorality to great comic effect. Without question, Anna is knowingly dangled before the Secretary to the Court as a key to improving family fortunes at the expense of her happiness and the pleasure of her lovelorn cousins. Her status as chattel is further underscored when she is unceremoniously returned to the Timoneda household following the shift in political winds at the palace. In light of her suddenly diminished market value, Juan is left to contemplate the impossibility of becoming a Brother of the Holy Blood, the stalled ascendance of Timoneda influence at court, and the insistence that his genius pander to the repressive agenda of the new local government.

All but one member of the Timoneda household are guilty of sacrificing personal beliefs for the illusion of profit and gain. Juan is all too eager to hand over Anna for a chance at social climbing and a virtual monopoly on printing, whereas Isabel (at least at first) calmly ticks off a list of commodities and favors she expects the Secretary to bestow upon the family as compensation for her niece's absence. A somewhat dimwitted but ultimately sympathetic character,

El señor de las patrañas (Rigmaroles)

Isabel is particularly disturbed by the sexual exploitation of Anna, and of all the characters in *Rigmaroles* she most eloquently voices the quandary of the powerless before their oppressors. The couple's younger son, Batista, poised to take over the family business, is likewise thrilled at any hint of favoritism or protection coming from the court. During Anna's visit home in Act Two, he presents her with a leather jewel box he has crafted for possible widespread (and exclusive) sale among the ladies at the palace. Only Vincent, who is clearly smitten with Anna and thus wracked by jealousy, maintains an uncompromising ethical perspective on the wisdom of forsaking strongly held values for money, power, or influence. An idealist and dreamer as his father once was, Vincent yearns to escape the family's straits and keeps his mind's eye focused on the elusive horizon beckoning him to undertake the romanticized voyage out he has been secretly planning for some time. Vincent's tenacious adherence to principle resolves several dilemmas simultaneously at play's end and prompts Juan to reconsider Timoneda family options absent the possibility of self-determination.

Upon hearing the news of the regime change at court, Juan correctly predicts that a period of religious oppression and cultural isolationism will follow, but he does not appear to understand the full effect of the new repressions until he learns, as Vincent has presciently warned him, that his original literary compositions will be compromised. Juan's reaction to this plight mirrors the limited options open to the Spanish people under another, more recent dictatorship, as high talk of maintaining one's dignity in the face of adversity and not capitulating to the aims of authoritarianism quickly devolves into a sense of fatalistic despondence. Juan quite literally suffers an adverse physical reaction to the thought of self-censorship before turning his confused anger against himself and his family: Batista watches in horror as his father sets fire to the print shop but manages to stave off total destruction as Juan gradually comes to his senses. *Rigmaroles* closes with Juan prepared to write the kind of religious drama the Secretary now requests for the upcoming city festival, which is followed by a rather extensive comic coda in verse affirming the ultimately compromised nature of existence. It is man's destiny to be a cuckold, whether because of honor or women. *Rigmaroles* depressingly suggests that, without the option of escape or flight, reluctant conformity to autocratic might is a foregone conclusion.

El otro William—The Other William

The Other William takes as its point of departure a question long debated by scholars of British literature to largely inconclusive ends, namely, whether William Shakespeare was actually the author of the works historically attributed to him. Salom pushes this infamous canard to great comic length, relying on the theatergoer's ready knowledge and easy grasp of the Bard's canon in peppering his play with a constant flow of Shakespearean allusion, often from improbable angles. The "Other William" of the play's title is William Stanley, the reluctant Sixth Earl of Derby, a closet dramatist who has little time or inclination to give his title of minor nobility and unkempt manorial grounds the fitting attention they observe. Untroubled by his relative impoverishment, William is content with his status as poor gentry as long as he can continue to write unencumbered, undisturbed, and undetected by his noble peers. His private métier, though, is irreversibly threatened by his arrogant brother's untimely death when, because of the caprices of aristocratic succession, the title of Sixth Earl is conferred on him. As a full-fledged but dispossessed noble (his brother's conniving widow has arranged for the ancestral assets and estate to be bequeathed to her daughters and so remain in her hands), William cannot risk the discredit that signing his own works would bring to his name. He thus contracts an actor in London by the name of "Shakpso or Shaksper" to take credit for the dramas and to have them staged. This sets in motion Salom's comic premise, as questions of authorship and originality are repeatedly called into play amid the ominous encroachment of "real-world" demands.

As with many of Salom's other historically based plays, much of the viewer's pleasure springs from noting the comedy's handling of subtle incongruities between fact and fiction. Thus, elements of all that is known of Shakespeare's life—a famously paltry biographical sketch—are included with less regard for historical veracity than for speculative force. *The Other William* suggests that Shakespeare was a mediocre actor and possibly a bisexual rogue who trained to be a glove maker and attended a small school in his native Stratford-on-Avon before fleeing to London to avoid possible imprisonment for deer poaching. Other scattershot data from various accounts of his life, for instance, that he was left-handed or enough of a dramatic imitator to be deemed "a bird who adorns himself in someone else's feathers," round out this jaundiced depiction of arguably the most famous writer in the English language. Indeed, Salom's extensive research in preparation for writing *The Other William* extends far beyond the shrouded life of Shakespeare to an intimate acquaintance with his vast body of work.

Strewn throughout the play, for instance, are lines and scenes from Shakespeare's most beloved dramas, whose provenience provides some of the

El otro William (The Other William)

work's most humorous moments. The audience learns that William Stanley is writing "a little play about a couple of youngsters who fall in love" that he might call "Romualdo and Juslinda." This comes after William's tardy servant, Costrand, has informed him: "It's the nightingale and not the lark that caresses [his] ear," hardly the only instance in which William is supplied with a line by an unlikely source. Even more outlandish is the overlapping of his life and his art, as when his sister-in-law, the Dowager, tells him: "I've heard about a Jew named Shylock who has made a fortune lending large sums to noblemen" or Shakespeare returns Lady Derby's handkerchief to William after a servant of the Earl of Essex retrieves it from the nobleman's bedchamber. Before the play concludes, mention is made—however fleetingly—of *Love's Labor's Lost, The Two Gentlemen of Verona, As You Like It, A Midsummer Night's Dream, Richard II, Macbeth, Julius Caesar, Henry IV,* and *The Tempest.* What's more, Yorick's skull (it is believed) sits all the while on a desk in William's castle.

Despite these obvious late English Renaissance trappings, *The Other William* is at heart concerned with the alienating aspects of authorship. Even while he is happiest, writing plays in enforced self-isolation from the world, William Stanley is "cruel and arrogant," disdainful of women in general, and cavalier toward the ministrations of his servant girl, Mary, in particular. Long before life's exigencies begin to close in on him—after assuming the station of the Sixth Earl of Derby, he is confronted with having to admit his authorship when *Richard II* sparks an antisedition riot—William is a failure as an enlightened human being, letting his estate go to weed, abusing his servant, Costrand, and using Mary flippantly to gratify his desires. As the Sixth Earl of Derby he ultimately loses Mary, experiences a disastrous political marriage, finds his reputation besmirched when his playwriting is exposed, and is left to face a court of law's imminent judgment against him. *The Other William* presents a strong case for the necessity of genius to thrive in seclusion, unperturbed by the impositions of the workaday world. The fragile tie connecting literary masterpieces to everyday life is left for the viewer to ponder.

Certainly, *The Other William* scrutinizes the intriguing question of artistic originality, reinforced in the play by Salom's use of doubling. Besides the parallel between the two Williams and the thematization of the porous frontiers between lived life and artistic product, *The Other William* takes advantage of fluid temporal and spatial planes. Thus, action that begins in the dramatic present with a guided tour through William Stanley's castle morphs seamlessly into the past with the same actor playing the guide suddenly portraying the Sixth Earl.

At another juncture, the actor in the role of Costrand steps out of character to don a judicial clerk's robe. Shakespeare, whom William Stanley has been paying to assume responsibility for authorship of the nobleman's plays, refuses to tell the court he is not their true author, rebuking the Sixth Earl for his neglect. "[Y]ou ignored your creatures like some superior and distant god while I, I modified scenes, corrected mistakes, cut here and added there. Perhaps you were the one who conceived them, but I cared for them as if they were my own children, I nurtured them and turned them into what they are," he protests, adding that he, "a humble actor," and Stanley, "a great lord," represent "two sides of a single coin." At Shakespeare's untimely death, Stanley admits, "I felt as if something of myself had died" before affirming that credit for his plays' authorship will remit without question to his own pen. Viewers of *The Other William* may well smirk at the statement's dramatic irony, however compelled they will feel to reconsider what it means to be a writer.

A PLAYWRIGHT'S FUTURE DIRECTIONS

Whether Jaime Salom will continue to entertain theatergoers and readers on both sides of the Atlantic with historical comedies remains an open question. His most recent plays, *Más o menos amigas* and *Las señoritas de Aviñón,* do, in fact, attest to a sustained interest in both comic and historical genres. It is also true that a considerable amount of his dramatic activity over the last decade or so has involved revising and reworking some of his earlier efforts. Whatever the case, with translations of no fewer than eleven of his plays now available in English, Salom is bound to enjoy increasing renown in America and the rest of the English-speaking world. With a career spanning nearly a half century and diverse works confounding facile encapsulation, Salom should have lovers of theater everywhere hoping that his future endeavors take drama, now in the twenty-first century, in still new and compelling directions.

Bibliography

PREMIERES OF ORIGINAL PLAYS BY JAIME SALOM

El mensaje [The Message]—Teatro Arriago, Bilbao. May 14, 1955.

El triángulo blanco [The White Triangle]—Teatro Guimerá, Barcelona. December 2, 1960.

Verde esmeralda [Emerald Green]—Teatro Alcázar, Madrid. December 12, 1960.

Culpables [The Guilty]—Teatro Reina Victoria, Madrid. August 8, 1961.

La gran aventura (in Catalan) [The Big Adventure]—Teatro Candilejas, Barcelona. November 24, 1961.

El baúl de los disfraces [The Trunk of Disguises]—Teatro Windsor, Barcelona. January 2, 1964.

Juegos de invierno [Winter Games]—Teatro Infanta Beatriz, Madrid. January 31, 1964.

El hombre del violín [The Man With the Violin]—Teatro Principal, Palma de Mallorca. February 7, 1964.

Falta de pruebas [Lack of Evidence]—Teatro Barcelona, Barcelona. September 16, 1964.

Espejo para dos mujeres [A Mirror for Two Women]—Teatro Windsor, Barcelona. September 20, 1965.

Parchís party [Parcheesi Party]—Teatro Valle Inclán, Madrid. December 4, 1965.

Cita los sábados [Saturday Night Date]—Teatro Candilejas, Barcelona. March 23, 1967.

La casa de las Chivas (The House of the Chivas)—Teatro Moratín, Barcelona. March 22, 1968.

Los delfines [The Heirs Apparent]—Teatro Calderón de la Barca, Barcelona. January 31, 1969.

La playa vacía (The Empty Beach)—Teatro Lara, Madrid. November 20, 1970.

Viaje en un trapecio [Trapeze Ride]—Teatro Moratín, Barcelona. November 27, 1970.

La noche de los cien pájaros [The Night of the Hundred Birds]—Teatro Marquina, Madrid. February 10, 1972.

Tiempo de espadas (Time of Swords)—Teatro Beatriz, Madrid. September 29, 1972.

Nueve brindis por un rey [Nine Toasts for a King]—Teatro Beatriz, Madrid. September 27, 1974.

La piel del limón (Bitter Lemon)—Teatro Marquina, Madrid. September 10, 1976.

Historias íntimas del paraíso (Behind the Scenes in Eden)—Teatro Marquina, Madrid. October 6, 1978.

El corto vuelo del gallo (The Cock's Short Flight)—Teatro Espronceda 34, Madrid. September 18, 1980.

Un hombre en la puerta [A Man at the Door]—Teatro Lara, Madrid. May 10, 1984.

Una hora sin televisión (One Hour Without Television)—Teatro Príncipe, Madrid. June 28, 1987.

Las Casas, una hoguera al amanecer (Bonfire at Dawn)—Teatro Jorge Negrete, Mexico City. August 3, 1990.

El señor de las patrañas (Rigmaroles)—Teatro Centro Cultural de la Villa, Madrid. October 19, 1990.

La lluna de Valencia (in Catalan) [The Moon Over Valencia]—Teatro Borras, Barcelona. October 29, 1992.

Casi una diosa (Almost a Goddess)—Teatro Bellas Artes, Madrid. February 4, 1993.

Mariposas negras [Black Butterflies]—Teatro Principal, Alicante. January 28, 1994.

Una noche con Clark Gable [A Night With Clark Gable]—Thalia Theater, New York City. February 11, 1994.

La trama [The Plot]—Teatro Juan Bravo, Segovia. November 8, 1996.

El otro William (The Other William)—Teatro Centro Cultural de la Villa, Madrid. January 23, 1998.

Más o menos amigas [Friends More or Less]—Teatro Reina Victoria, Madrid. August 17, 1999.

Las señoritas de Aviñón [The Demoiselles of Avignon]—Teatro Jaime Salom, Parla. February 17, 2001.

En la pecera [In the Fishbowl]—Biblioteca del Alcázar, Toledo. January 23, 2002.

Esta noche no hay cine [No Movies Tonight]—Teatro Jaime Salom, Parla. November 19, 2003.

PLAYS BY JAIME SALOM TRANSLATED INTO ENGLISH

Almost a Goddess. Trans. Gwynne Edwards. *Burning the Curtain: Four Revolutionary Spanish Plays.* London: Marion Boyars, 1995, 205–254. Trans. of *Casi una diosa.*

Behind the Scenes in Eden. Trans. Marion Peter Holt. Selected scenes in *Literary Review* 36.3 (1993): 398–411. Trans. of *Historias íntimas del paraíso.*

Bitter Lemon. Trans. Patricia W. O'Connor. *Plays of the New Democratic Spain (1975–1990).* Ed. Patricia W. O'Connor. Lanham, MD: University Press of America, 1992, 103–164. Trans. of *La piel del limón.*

Bonfire at Dawn. Trans. Phyllis Zatlin. University Park, PA: ESTRENO, 1992. Trans. of *Las Casas, una hoguera al amanecer.*

The Cock's Short Flight. Trans. Marion Peter Holt. *DramaContemporary: Spain.* Ed. Marion Peter Holt. New York: Performing Arts Journal Publications, 1985, 139–190. Trans. of *El corto vuelo del gallo.*

UNPUBLISHED

The Empty Beach. Trans. Jack Agüeros. Trans. of *La playa vacía.*

The House of the Chivas. Trans. Barbara Carballal. Trans. of *La casa de las Chivas.*

One Hour Without Television. Trans. Jack Agüeros. Trans. of *Una hora sin televisión.*

Time of Swords. Trans. Marion Peter Holt. Trans. of *Tiempo de espadas.*

FULL-LENGTH STUDIES OF THE WORKS OF JAIME SALOM

Izquierdo Gómez, Jesús. *Conformación y éxito de un dramaturgo: Jaime Salom.* Granada: Universidad de Granada, 1997.

————. *Obra teatral de Jaime Salom*. Granada: Universidad de Granada, 1993.

Marqueríe, Alfredo. *Realidad y fantasía en el teatro de Jaime Salom*. Madrid: Escelicer, 1973.

Zatlin-Boring, Phyllis. *Jaime Salom*. Twayne's World Authors Series 588. Boston: G. K. Hall, 1982.

SELECTED ESSAYS IN ENGLISH ON
THE THEATER OF JAIME SALOM

Holt, Marion P. "Jaime Salom." *The Contemporary Spanish Theater (1949–1972)*. Boston: G. K. Hall, 1975, 156–159.

————. "*Tiempo de espadas*: Salom's Religio-Political Dramatic Testament." *ESTRENO* 8.2 (1982): 19–20.

Klein, Dennis A. "Epic Theater of the Conquest: Jaime Salom's *Las Casas. Una hoguera en el amanecer* and Peter Shaffer's *The Royal Hunt of the Sun*." *ESTRENO* 18.2 (1992): 34–36.

Zatlin, Phyllis. "The Discovery of the New World and National Identity: Theatrical Perspectives of Gala and Salom." *España Contemporánea* 12.2 (1999): 95–102.

————. "Twentieth-Century Spanish Theater on the American Stage." *Theater Survey* 42.1 (2001): 69–84.

————. "Two-Character Plays as 'Teatro íntimo': Examples From Díaz, Junyent, and Salom." *España Contemporánea* 4.1 (1991): 97–102.

Zatlin-Boring, Phyllis. "Expressionism in the Contemporary Spanish Theater." *Modern Drama* 26.3 (1983): 555–569.

————. "Jaime Salom and the Use of Doubling." *American Hispanist* 4.34–35 (1979): 11–14.

About the Translations

JAIME SALOM'S REPUTATION as an assiduous reviser of his dramas is assuredly deserved, so it is of special interest to scholars and students of theater (as well as of translation) to note which editions of his plays serve as source texts for versions rendered into other languages. In most cases, as might be expected, Salom's revisions are principally of the stylistic and structural kind, constituted by the usual paring of speeches, tightening of dialogue, and smoother integration of minor characters and subplots. In a few instances, however, Salom's reworking of a drama has proved substantial enough for the play to be restaged under a new title. This was the case with *Parchís party* [Parcheesi Party] (1965), which became *Cita los sábados,* whereas the early crime drama *Falta de pruebas* [Lack of Evidence] (1964) was revised as *La noche de los cien pájaros.* Similarly, *Culpables* has enjoyed a second incarnation as *La trama* [The Plot] (1996), and Salom reworked *Una noche con Clark Gable* into *Más o menos amigas.*

Marion Peter Holt's *Behind the Scenes in Eden* is based on the original playscript of *Historias íntimas del paraíso* with additional cuts the author made in preparation for the play's French edition. G. J. Racz's *Rigmaroles* uses as its source text the revised version of *El señor de las patrañas* published by the *Sociedad*

General de Autores de España (Madrid, 1992), and the similarly revised *Fundamentos* edition of *El otro William* (Madrid, 1998) serves as the basis for Phyllis Zatlin's *The Other William*. In all three cases, the translators followed the playwright's wishes in using the original Spanish texts he requested for this first American collection of his plays.

Behind the Scenes in Eden
(Historias íntimas del paraíso)

A Farce in Two Acts by Jaime Salom

Translated by Marion Peter Holt

Characters

ANGEL

ADAM

LILI

EVE

Act I

A lush, leafy corner of Eden. The Angel, dressed very conservatively in a black coat and pinstriped trousers, resembles a hotel manager. He is saying goodbye to someone who has just climbed into a helicopter, as if the machine were taking off from the orchestra of the theater.

ANGEL: Goodbye, have a good trip, congratulations! It's gorgeous! A masterpiece. Best of luck!

(The noise of the motor grows louder, forcing him to shout and wave his arms.)

Masterpiece! I said it's a masterpiece! The finest you've created to date, truly the finest. I said it's the finest! And thank you, thank you very much for the trust you've shown me, assigning me to this post. Thank you! No! Nothing! Thank youuuuu! And have a good weekend, Lord. Goodbye. Goodbyeeee!

(A lot of wind, and the noise of the motor fades away. Angel goes on waving. Suddenly all is silence, and he stands alone, at a loss.)

Now what? This is all very comfortable. He's always building, creating, dabbling with clay. . . . I have to admit it turned out quite well. Very pretty, everything in place. But who's going to take charge of conservation and maintenance? You can turn things out on the assembly line, but then who's to keep them running? While He's up there having a divine rest, I'm down here with all the responsibilities. And I don't even know the names of all these things.

(He puts on a pair of reading glasses and picks up one of the books.)

Let's see what he calls the place . . . "parachute," "parade," "paradise." That's it, paradise. I'm the District Manager of Paradise. Not as boring as the Office of Statistics and Records, I suppose. I had my fill of that. So, foolish me, I applied for this job, but . . . Hey, you. Whatever you're called . . . you! Damn it. *(He consults the book again.)* "Mammary," "mammal. . . ." All these technical terms! Ah, here it is . . . "man." I mustn't forget. Man. Hey, you, man. Come over here!

ADAM: *(Entering, wearing only faded jeans and a T-shirt.)* You mean me?

ANGEL: Who else? You're the only one around.

ADAM: But you called me a funny name.

ANGEL: "Man." I called you "man." Let's see if you can learn the word. You have to keep up with the nomenclature. You can call me Angel.

ADAM: Angel. I'll try to remember.

ANGEL: I'm actually an archangel, but since there're just the two of us around, we might as well dispense with formality.

ADAM: So, what can I do for you, Mr. Angel?

ANGEL: Just relax. Don't confuse me with a lot of questions.
(Pause. Adam looks at him with utter calm. Angel is ill at ease.)
I suppose you don't know anything about all this, do you?

ADAM: I just arrived.

ANGEL: So you did . . .

ADAM: I thought you were the one who was supposed to have all the facts.

ANGEL: Of course. That's why I'm here. To give you the facts.

ADAM: I'm glad of that. I feel so out of it. *(Another pause.)* What do you call that?

ANGEL: What?

ADAM: That long stick with green hair. *(He points to a tree.)*

ANGEL: Well . . . *(Reacting.)* Please, you can't learn everything at once. One thing at a time. Don't be impatient. Besides, the "stick" with green hair doesn't concern you.

ADAM: I just wanted to know . . . out of curiosity.

ANGEL: Well, wait a moment. . . . *(He leafs through the book again.)*

ADAM: It caught my eye. . . . It's so . . . so . . .

ANGEL: *(Still searching.)* So what?

ADAM: So dreamy.

ANGEL: What *are* you talking about?

ADAM: The green hair.

ANGEL: Will you forget about the confounded hair? Once you get an idea in your head . . . I forbid you to talk about hair again. Understood?

ADAM: Understood, Mr. Angel.

ANGEL: *(Finding what he was looking for at last.)* Tree. The stupid thing is called a tree.

ADAM: What stupid thing?

ANGEL: The one with the green hair.

ADAM: Tree. That's pretty. *(He goes around touching the different trees.)* Hello, tree. How are you, tree? How are things with you, tree?

ANGEL: Enough of that.

ADAM: What do we do now?

ANGEL: Whatever you wish. You can walk over there and then go in the opposite direction. . . . Oh, I don't know. Do whatever comes into your mind.

ADAM: Okay. *(He takes a very short walk.)* I'm getting bored.

ANGEL: You'll have to learn to live with it. If you think you've come into the world just to have a good time . . .

ADAM: Then why have I come?

ANGEL: I don't know, my boy. It's too early to say. Time will tell.
(Pause.)

ADAM: Were you born today, too?

ANGEL: *(Feeling superior.)* I? Please . . . I've put in many hours of flying time. If I told you how many centuries I've been around.

ADAM: You're very well preserved.

ANGEL: I can't complain.

ADAM: Have you always lived here?

ANGEL: Really, now! They've just transferred me. I was in the central Office of Statistics and Records. Division of Star Affairs. Satellite Department.

ADAM: It must be a very nice place.

ANGEL: That depends. . . . I spent centuries making mathematical calculations.

ADAM: Why?

ANGEL: Well, I don't really know. Everyone does his job there without asking questions. We used logarithms to calculate the orbits and velocities in light years.

ADAM: For what?

ANGEL: To record them. Then we sent the data to the head office, and they put it all on tape.

ADAM: What did they do with it?

ANGEL: How would I know? If you want to get along, keep a low profile and don't ask too many questions. If I told you what happened to some friends of mine who wanted to know everything and went on strike up there, you wouldn't believe it. They hushed it up in a hurry.

ADAM: You couldn't have had much fun.

ANGEL: It was a terrible drag.

ADAM: If you've just arrived here, I imagine you don't know too much about all this . . .

ANGEL: Don't be impudent! I know all there is to know. Do you think I got the job through somebody else's influence?

ADAM: *(After another pause.)* I'm still bored.

ANGEL: Well, go take another stroll. . . .

ADAM: Why don't you come with me? Maybe two can have more fun than one.

ANGEL: I have a lot to do . . . but all right, just to satisfy you. . . .

> *(They start to walk around.)*

> How's it going?

ADAM: *(Spiritless.)* So-so.

ANGEL: You're too restless. If you don't change you're going to have a hard time dealing with eternity.

> *(Sound of bleating.)*

ADAM: Hey, what's that?

ANGEL: How absentminded I've become! I completely forgot.

ADAM: What?

ANGEL: I put them in a pen so they wouldn't soil my clothes. Come look. *(He pushes aside some branches and points to something in the distance.)*

ADAM: Ohhhh! What funny-looking trees.

ANGEL: They aren't trees, stupid. They're animals.

ADAM: They can even move around.

ANGEL: That's the objectionable part. They move all over the place and leave everything a total wreck.

ADAM: And they're all different. Look at the cute one with long ears. And the big one with a funny nose. And the one with all the fluffy padding. What do you call them?

ANGEL: Each one has a different name. It's very complicated. Take the book and find out for yourself if you're all that interested. There's a complete inventory. *(To the animals.)* All right, all right! Just keep it down. Relax! What a hassle!

ADAM: Lend me your glasses. I won't be able to read without them.

ANGEL: *(He hands them to Adam.)* Some job I've got!

> *(He exits. Adam sits on the ground, puts on the glasses, and begins to read.)*

ADAM: Two tigers. . . . Two rabbits. . . . Two giraffes, two dinosaurs. . . . Two . . . *(He starts turning pages.)* There are two of everything. . . . *(He looks at himself, very unique and very single, and lets out a cry.)* Angel! Angel!

ANGEL: *(Entering all out of breath.)* What's wrong?

ADAM: Nothing. I wanted to ask you a question.

ANGEL: You gave me a scare! Do you know what those crazy animals are up to now? ... Come look. Do you see? Some of them are climbing on top of the others.

ADAM: That's stupid. Why would they do that?

ANGEL: I haven't the slightest idea. Maybe they just got tangled up.

ADAM: Maybe one of them wants to be on top to get a better view of the horizon.

ANGEL: I tried to help some of the poor things get down, and you should have seen how angry they got.

ADAM: I don't get it. There's obviously plenty of room for all of them. No need to stack up like that.

ANGEL: Look. Some of them are getting down. There doesn't seem to be any damage.

ADAM: They look absolutely blissful.

ANGEL: It's a mystery to me. I don't understand it at all.

ADAM: It's beyond me, too. *(Transition.)* Mr. Angel, I'd like to ask you something ... out of curiosity. Nothing important ... you'll probably think it's trivial.

ANGEL: Well, if it's so trivial, would you mind waiting until later? I'm awfully busy.

ADAM: I've been looking at your book ... and then I saw what was going on behind the fence. And I realized that all the animals come in pairs.

ANGEL: It's a detail that caught my eye, too. Why would there be two of every species? It looks like one would have been sufficient.

ADAM: Maybe to have a spare ... just in case one breaks down. There would always be one left.

ANGEL: That seems a reasonable explanation.

ADAM: Okay, now listen. . . . Why have they created only one of me? If I had company, maybe I'd have more fun.

ANGEL: Thanks a lot. Do you find my company all that unbearable?

ADAM: No, Mr. Angel. . . . You're very nice, but it would be something different. Don't you see?

ANGEL: What made you think they'd made you different from all the rest? That's ridiculous. You, too, have a spare.

ADAM: You mean . . . ?

ANGEL: Exactly. There's another man, just like you.

ADAM: *(Delighted.)* You don't say! Where is he?

ANGEL: Well, at the moment I can't quite remember . . . but it will come to me. The Lord made two of you at the same time. I saw it with my own eyes. From the same clay. Two balls of mud and presto, presto, plam, plam . . . first the head, then the arms and legs . . . and there you have the finished product. Then He sealed you both in plastic so the sun wouldn't dry you out. I haven't unwrapped the other one yet. He's still in the package. Now where the devil did I put him?

ADAM: *(In an outburst.)* How can you forget something that important! You're . . . incompetent.

ANGEL: That's the limit. Just who do you think you are?

ADAM: The owner of all this, I suppose.

ANGEL: Nobody's made you the owner. It's been lent to you . . . you only have the use of the property.

ADAM: And as for you, you're only my administrator. So show me a little more respect, please.

ANGEL: *(Flushed with anger.)* Just hope He's not watching! And thank your lucky stars I'm an angel and not . . . Be careful; even though I may not look it, I've got a low boiling point. *(Transition.)* But let me think.

ADAM: What's he like?

ANGEL: Like you. I already told you that. Identical. Like two drops of water. Ah, now it's coming back. I know where I put him.

ADAM: Where? My curiosity's killing me.

ANGEL: Behind those bushes. Help me clear them away.

ADAM: I can't wait.

ANGEL: Stop it. You're making a mess of everything. Leave it to me.
(Angel separates some branches and reveals The Woman, *seated smiling, motionless as a beautiful statue, in a big cellophane globe like an enormous Easter egg. She is dressed exactly like Adam.)*

ADAM: *(His excitement growing.)* Look at him! Just look at him!

ANGEL: Yes, my boy. I see. Help me. *(They move the globe to center stage.)*

ADAM: Did you ever see anything as pretty as that? My God, what a treat!

ANGEL: Will you calm down!

ADAM: Nothing missing. Two little eyes. Two little ears. All those little fingers. Look . . . he's not exactly like me. There are differences. . . .

ANGEL: You think so?

ADAM: Look closely. The hair, for example. His is long and mine's short.

ANGEL: That's true.

ADAM: And those lumps he has in front. Touch me. Go ahead, touch me. Flat, utterly flat.

ANGEL: You're right. How curious.

ADAM: But I like him even if he's not perfect. I really, really, really like him. It's a miracle. We have to have a celebration.

ANGEL: That's enough. I'm going to lose my patience. It's only another creation. A newer model, to be sure, but nothing more.

ADAM: Will you take him out of the package for me?

ANGEL: And what if he starts creating a nuisance or wants to climb on top of you, like those?

ADAM: Whatever he takes a notion to do, I'll bear it patiently. Be a good Angel and open the package.

ANGEL: All right . . . but don't make me responsible for the consequences.

ADAM: I promise. Yes, yes, yes, yes.

(He claps his hands like a child, running around the package enthusiastically. Angel opens the cellophane egg. The Woman inside immediately moves normally.)

WOMAN: Hello. Good morning. Thank you for getting me out of there. It was awfully stuffy inside, sealed up like that. Sometimes you feel the need to stretch your legs. *(To Angel.)* You're Angel, aren't you? *(Shaking hands.)* Delighted to meet you. And you're Adam, right? *(She kisses him on the cheek.)* Happy to know you. I'm your wife.

ADAM: My what?

WOMAN: Or you're my husband, as you prefer. Of course, the whole thing is absolutely grotesque. A marriage like this by royal edict, without ever having met. It can't be for real.

ADAM: But . . . aren't you a man like me?

WOMAN: *(Laughing.)* Really, do I have a man's face? Quite the contrary. I'm a female. Or a lady or a woman, whichever you prefer. And I'm proud of it!

ADAM: What's your name?

WOMAN: What's my name going to be? Lili.

ANGEL & ADAM: Lili?

LILI: Yes, Lili. What's so surprising about that? Such pretty flowers and how nice they smell. I love springtime. I have to confess . . . I'm a romantic at heart. *(She has put some flowers in her hair.)* Do they suit me?

ADAM: Well . . .

LILI: It's wonderful to see the trees so full of blooms. Cherry trees, chestnut trees, almond trees . . .

ADAM: How do you know what trees are?

LILI: It's simple. You just open your eyes and use your head.

ADAM: Have you been here before?

LILI: You talk as if you didn't know I've just been created. Like you. At the same moment and from the same clay. We're twins. Which does make our marriage a bit different. It's not that I'm narrow-minded; but, after all, a marriage between brother and sister, children of the same father. . . . But it's probably only one of those absurd taboos anyhow. Who knows . . . ?

ANGEL: Who taught you all this?

LILI: Me? Why, I've never been outside that cocoon. But one observes and reflects. Besides, I'm a woman.

ANGEL: What's that got to do with it?

LILI: By the way, Angel love, where can I find the Lord?

ANGEL: For what?

LILI: There are a few things I'd like to tell Him.

ANGEL: Impossible. He's resting. No one can bother Him now. That's why I'm here. What do you want?

LILI: For the moment, just show me how to file a complaint.

ANGEL: And what do you have to complain about?

LILI: A list of things this long. To begin with, they married me off without giving it any thought. Picked at random. Did any one ask me, "Lili dear, what kind of man would you like for a husband? Tall, short, fat, skinny, bald, hairy, white or black?" And what if I preferred a redskin, for example? Well, bear up, Lili, and be satisfied with what you get. Forgive me, Adam, nothing personal intended.

ADAM: Then you don't find me attractive.

LILI: That has nothing to do with it. Doesn't it irk you that they plan your whole life without even consulting you?

ANGEL: You're getting me all confused. How could he choose another woman if there wasn't one? Or you another man if he's the only one in existence?

LILI: Since we were made to order, at least they could have inquired about our preferences.

ANGEL: How dare you talk this way!

LILI: When you got married, I suppose . . .

ANGEL: *(Red with anger.)* I've never been married. I'm an angel. I'm sufficient unto myself; I'm more than sufficient unto myself.

LILI: I beg your pardon. I didn't mean to offend you.

ANGEL: I'm very proud of being as I am.

LILI: You're certainly a very attractive Angel, but don't you ever get tired of being alone?

ANGEL: Never. I have a seraphic character, and I always have a divine time.

LILI: Well, now that we've settled that. . . . What ideas do you have on the topic of sex?

ADAM & ANGEL: What??

LILI: Don't you even know what it is?

ADAM: I haven't the slightest idea.

LILI: I'll have to find a way to explain it. . . . Sex is . . . what's underneath your zipper. Surely you've had enough curiosity to pull it down and see how it works.

ADAM: Ah . . . does this go up and down?

LILI: Yes, my boy, it goes up and down . . . depending on the occasion. *(She turns away from the audience.)* You see? This way. *(She opens and closes her zipper.)*

ADAM: *(Jumping up and down deliriously.)* Oh, oh, some view!

ANGEL: What's come over him?

LILI: *(To Adam.)* Now take a look at yourself.

ADAM: Me? I don't dare.

LILI: Nothing's going to bite you. Go on.

ADAM: *(With much modesty and turning his back to everyone.)* Oh, my goodness, what's all this? It's ugly. Somebody made a mistake, Angel. The Lord must have been overworked. He botched me up.

ANGEL: It can't be that bad.

ADAM: If you saw what's hanging from me. It's embarrassing.

LILI: You're perfectly normal, Adam. There are certain differences . . . fortunately for both of us.

ANGEL: I don't see the point of it.

LILI: Adam, did they ask you by chance what sex you wanted?

ADAM: Not me.

LILI: Me either. As you can see, they haven't consulted either of us on the most elemental things. It's outrageous . . .

ANGEL: *(Fed up.)* Enough! This is getting out of hand. From now on you can learn to grin and bear it.
(Pause.)

ADAM: How about you . . . don't you have anything hanging in front?

ANGEL: I have too many things on my mind to worry about such nonsense.

ADAM: Wouldn't you like to find out?

ANGEL: No!

ADAM: But it's bothering me. I can't be normal. Would it be too much trouble for you to take a quick look?

ANGEL: On the condition that we don't discuss it anymore. Agreed?

ADAM: Agreed.

ANGEL: That's settled. *(He turns his back to the audience.)* You see?

ADAM: I sure do, and there's nothing there at all!

LILI: Of course not because he's an angel.

ANGEL: I'm delighted that there's nothing. Delighted and happy. Besides, if you want my opinion, I find it much more pleasing, aesthetically speaking. In any case, the matter's closed.

ADAM: Closed. *(Adam begins to laugh.)*

ANGEL: Now what's so amusing?

ADAM: Nothing. It just strikes me as funny. That there are three of us, and in this one detail we're totally incompatible. *(He laughs again.)*

ANGEL: I'm losing my patience. Is this the only topic of conversation? The Lord has created the highest mountains, thousands of acres of forests, millions of species of every order, snow, rain, volcanoes . . . but not a word about those marvels. Obviously, the only thing that concerns you is an insignificant little thing, this big, that I never heard discussed once in the Home Office in all the centuries I've worked there. And believe me, they keep the measurements of everything of any real importance in the universe. You disappoint me.

LILI: If they've never even talked about it where you've been, what kind of sex education are we going to get?

ANGEL: There are more urgent matters to concern us. Besides, I have some booklets that explain everything. *(He goes to the table to look for them.)* This is the Garden of Eden, the most recent creation of the Supreme Maker. One of His most perfect achievements, and completed in the record time of six days. As we know, the Maker is the author of such well-known masterpieces as the Sun, the Moon, and the Milky Way. . . .

ADAM: *(Walking around Lili.)* Pretty, pretty, pretty. Pretty!

ANGEL: What's wrong with him?

LILI: I think he likes me.

ADAM: Very much.

LILI: Well, you aren't so bad yourself.

ANGEL: *(Who doesn't understand any of this.)* I've never heard such inane conversation. If you're so bored with each other, one of you can take a walk in that direction, and the other one can go in the opposite direction.

ADAM: Me bored? I should say not!

LILI: Neither am I.

ANGEL: But a moment ago you were telling me . . .

ADAM: I'm having a wonderful time.

LILI: It *is* rather pleasant here, isn't it?

ADAM: Sensational.

ANGEL: *(Continues reading the prospectus.)* Under your feet, the earth; over your heads, the sky . . . also called the Firmament by scientists, which has the curious characteristic of changing color according to the time of day.

LILI: Listen, I suddenly feel very hungry. *(To Adam.)* Don't you?

ADAM: I don't know what "hungry" means.

LILI: The urge to eat. . . . *(Demonstrating. Picking an apple.)* Can I pick the fruit?

ANGEL: Everything is for your use. But why bother? It looks so pretty where it is.

LILI: *(After taking a bite.)* It's delicious. *(To Adam.)* Would you like a bite?

ADAM: *(Fearful.)* What do I do with it?

LILI: You swallow it. Like this. Mmmmmm. Try it.

ADAM: *(Bites.)* What do I do now?

LILI: Close your teeth. How do you like it?

ADAM: *(Spitting it out with a great display.)* Ufff. How nauseating. It's cold and sour. I don't like it at all.

LILI: But it's delicious. *(To Angel.)* What do you call this marvel?

ANGEL: I know the word, I know it. It's right on the tip of my tongue, but at the moment . . . *(Grabs a book.)* "Almond, apricot . . . apple." "Apple!" That's it. . . .

LILI: Thank you. I really love apples. *(To Angel.)* Want a taste?

ANGEL: I have no need for such rubbish. I neither eat nor drink. I'm a very pure spirit, and don't forget it. Apple . . . why does that word ring a bell?

LILI: Can you reach another one for me? *(Angel obliges.)*

ADAM: *(Who has pulled up a carrot and is gnawing on it.)* This is a lot better. You should try it.

ANGEL: Forgetful me! Now I remember. It's even in the prospectus. Lili, I'm sorry, but you can't eat apples.

LILI: Why not?

ANGEL: I don't know, but you can't. It's strictly forbidden. It seems that the tree is under some kind of curse. It's called the Tree of Good and Evil.

LILI: Evil?

ANGEL: *(Handing her the prospectus and the glasses.)* Here, read it for yourself.

LILI: *(Putting on the glasses and reading.)* "The inhabitants will be able to enjoy all the services and installations, eat and drink whatever they wish, except apples." I can't believe it.

ANGEL: There you have it. I didn't make it up.

LILI: It must be a typographical error.

ANGEL: But Lili . . .

LILI: Take a good look at what I'm doing with this little apple. *(She eats.)*

ADAM: Lili, eat something else. What's the difference? This is delicious.

LILI: I don't want anything else.

ANGEL: Do it for me. If they find out up there, they'll remove me from this post and send me back to Statistics.

ADAM: I won't put up with your whims. *(He takes the apple from her.)*

LILI: *(Taking it back.)* I'm eating the fruit on principle, not for any whim. A few hours ago, what was I? Nothing. Zero. Suddenly, the Lord comes up with the wild idea of creating me, and here I am. Without consulting me, of course. Then they put me in this promised land called Paradise. But right off they come out with: you can eat this but not that; you can walk here but not there. Will you tell me what kind of bad joke life is?

ANGEL: There will always be prohibitions and commandments.

LILI: Why?

ANGEL: Do you know what you are, Lili? An ingrate.

LILI: No, Angel, I'm not. I think I'd like to live here and breathe this pure air, listen to the birds, and look at all that up there . . . What's it called?

ANGEL: The heavens.

LILI: That's it. And this down here, the earth. I think I'm going to be enthusiastic about all of it . . . but I'm also going to be enthusiastic about Lili. If I weren't, then you really could call me an ingrate for not appreciating the Lord's generosity. *(Transition.)* And now, with your permission I'm going over to the lake. *(To Angel.)* Do you have any bubble bath?

ANGEL: I'm afraid it hasn't been invented yet.

LILI: Very well. I'll manage without it. . . .

ADAM: Be careful. There's a lot of water. Don't drown yourself.

LILI: And yes, I'm also enthusiastic about Adam. I don't say he's handsome, but in his own way he's quite impressive. *(She exits.)*

ADAM: *(Very excited.)* Did you hear? She likes me, she likes me. . . . *(He kisses Angel on both cheeks.)* Oh, Angel, how I love you! *(He exits, running after Lili.)*

ANGEL: *(Wiping his cheek.)* Uuffff! This fellow's going to pose problems. And the other one's just as bad. What a pair! Oh, Angel, if God doesn't lend a hand, I'll see you back in Statistics and Records very soon.
(Fadeout. Music.)

Act 1

SCENE 2

When the lights come up, it is night. Lili is eating an apple and reading like mad by candlelight. She's using glasses, as everyone does when reading these books. A few moments later Adam enters.

ADAM: Still studying?

LILI: What else can I do? Angel is a dear, but he doesn't give very clear answers. By the way, where is he now?

ADAM: Struggling with the animals. Trying to keep them lined up and going where he says, as if they were satellites. I've brought you some flowers.

LILI: Thank you. I pulled up this carrot for you.

ADAM: It's stupendous. *(Pointing to the books.)* Have you learned anything?

LILI: A lot of things. Now I understand why God is so famous. What a talent! Everything fits perfectly, like an incredible puzzle He puts together piece by piece. He must be unique!

ADAM: You're an intellectual.

LILI: If we're going to live here all our lives, I want to be informed. Doesn't it interest you?

ADAM: I find reading very boring.

LILI: This invention of man and woman can work marvelously well, you know, but it's so carefully equilibrated that when one of them tugs the cord too hard, the whole thing can be wrecked in a moment. Fortunately, God has created an aid called "love."

ADAM: Love. That's a nice-sounding word. How can you recognize love when you see it?

LILI: Well, it seems that lovers hold hands, sigh, look into each other's eyes in the moonlight, and other more complicated things I'll tell you about.

ADAM: *(Taking her hand.)* Listen, do you know that looking into your eyes in the moonlight makes me feel sort of . . . speechless?

LILI: Yes, Adam, it does make you feel sort of speechless.
(They both sigh.)

ADAM: You have to admit that the Lord got it right when He created love. *(Breaking the mood, very euphoric.)* Now what about the other things?

LILI: I knew you'd get around to asking sooner or later.

ADAM: They must be sensational.

LILI: Yes, they must be.

ADAM: At this moment I'm having some very strange reactions.

LILI: I am, too, in my own way.

ADAM: Have you managed to find out how all this fits together?

LILI: I've even taken some notes in case we run into a snag.

ADAM: Maybe I could like certain kinds of books.

LILI: Adam, kiss me.

ADAM: Kiss. Another nice word.
  (Lili kisses him.)

LILI: The world's first kiss. Don't you find it stirring?

ADAM: *(Kissing her repeatedly like a madman.)* The world's second kiss, the third, the fourth, and the world's fifth kiss!

LILI: We're the luckiest couple in history because we aren't imitating anybody; we invent it all for ourselves: kissing, love . . .

ADAM: Taking baths . . . I'm happy, happy, happy!

LILI: And for the first time we're going to copulate.

ADAM: Do what?

LILI: That . . .

ADAM: Oh, of course, that . . .

LILI: If you don't like the idea.

ADAM: Of course I like the idea, yes, I do . . . but would you lend me your notes?

LILI: And the glasses so you can see better.
  (He looks at the notes.)

ADAM: How awful!

LILI: It may shock you at first, but you'll get used to the idea right away.

ADAM: And some idea! I'd never have thought of it in a hundred years. *(With slowly growing enthusiasm.)* It's fascinating, it's exciting . . . it's colossal! Go on, stretch out, beautiful, I'm ready.

LILI: What do you mean "stretch out"?

ADAM: Pull down your zipper and lie there quietly on the ground so I can see if I've got the first step right.

LILI: And where do *you* plan to be?

ADAM: Well, on top, of course. On top of you.

LILI: And me on the bottom.

ADAM: Naturally.

LILI: Naturally my foot.

ADAM: One of us has to be on top.

LILI: Why you?

ADAM: Why not me? Look, let's just give it a go. If two things are superimposed, one of them has to be on top. That's logic.

LILI: So what?

ADAM: Just shut up and do what I say.

LILI: Ha, ha, ha, harah, harah . . .

ADAM: What?

LILI: Of if you prefer, dippydippy, dippydippy . . .*(She gives him a Bronx cheer.)*

ADAM: Speak English. I don't know any foreign languages.

LILI: In matters of love there are no generals and no soldiers. We both have the same rank. We're equals . . .

ADAM: Look, don't get me angry. You and I will never be equals. I'm stronger and taller than you.

LILI: Ah, if it's a question of size . . . but I'm better educated.

ADAM: I weigh more.

LILI: I'm cleverer.

ADAM: And I'm more macho!

LILI: Then I'm more woman!

ADAM: Nobody can reason with you.

LILI: Silly, this argument could go on for centuries. . . . Let's stop bickering and just be happy.

ADAM: *(Reacting after a short pause.)* You think you're very smart, don't you? Three little words, a smile, and you settle everything to suit you.

LILI: But it's written in the books.

ADAM: I've had my fill of your confounded books. They're to blame for everything that's happened. You read some fancy words, and now you believe you're the queen of the Universe! It's time for a change, Lili. Now you'll see what I'm going to do to that pile of cheap literature.

LILI: What are you planning to do?

ADAM: Rip them into shreds . . . this tiny.

LILI: Don't be stupid. The Lord wrote them. Angel! Angel!

ADAM: *(With a book in his hand.)* "Planning for the Human Family." This is what I think of planning. To hell with the human family! *(He tears it apart.)*

LILI: No, you can't do that. Angel! Angel!
(Angel enters, running.)

ANGEL: What's going on?

LILI: Look.

ADAM: "Practical Guide for Sexual Justice." See where sexual justice is going? *(He rips it apart, too.)*

ANGEL: What are you doing, idiot?

ADAM: "Woman," "Women's Rights," "Male-Female Equality." *(He goes on destroying them.)*

ANGEL: Have you taken leave of your senses? *(Forcibly restraining him.)* That's enough! I'll have you thrown out! Just be glad I'm not authorized to liquidate anyone . . . but if I decide to pick up that phone, they'll send special agents.

ADAM: And now for the glasses. Where are those damn glasses?

ANGEL: *(Grabbing the glasses and trying to fend him off.)* No, not the glasses!

LILI: Really, Adam, will you stop acting like a child!

ADAM: Me, a child? I'll have you know I'm not a child and I never have been. And when I need books about women, sex, or any other trivial matters, I'll write them myself!

ANGEL: Heavens above! How am I going to get things to run smoothly again? They're going to demote me for sure, send me to rehabilitation camp . . .

LILI: *(To Adam.)* Are you satisfied now? The stupid things men will do to prove they're men.

ADAM: Just shut up. You've caused enough trouble already.

LILI: Me?

ADAM: With your brazen, rebellious attitude.

LILI: You're unfair!

ADAM: It would be much easier for you to agree with me. And more comfortable, too, I assure you. I'd bring home the food, and you wouldn't have to leave the house. I'd let you go first and hold the door. I'd even write poetry to you. . . . I'd place you on an altar.

LILI: Thanks, but I prefer to open my doors and walk on my own two feet.

ANGEL: Oh dear, oh dear! *(He tries to fit the pieces of the books back together.)*

LILI: Look. Not a one is still in one piece. *(She laughs.)* What a dope you are!

ADAM: *(Laughing too.)* Well, I guess I sort of flew off the handle . . .

LILI: Over nothing. Why are you men so silly?

ADAM: You're stubborn. Why are women so hardheaded? *(He stands there looking at her.)*

LILI: Don't stare at me that way. I must look a fright.

ADAM: Oh, no. You're very pretty. Cross my heart.

LILI: I don't believe you.

    (They hold hands.)

ADAM: What was that silly word we were arguing about? Copu . . . what?

LILI: Copulate. I hope you didn't tear up the notes I made, too.

ADAM: I put them in my pocket . . . just in case.

LILI: Do you know what this is called? Reconciliation.

ADAM: Another nice word: reconciliation.

    (They go off slowly with their arms around each other.)

ANGEL: Where are they going? If I leave them alone, they'll kill each other. *(He follows them.)* What are they doing now? A moment ago they were fighting like cats and dogs, and now they're making love. And just look how they're doing it! That's a new way! Nobody will ever understand human beings. Well, I suppose I should thank heaven for small blessings.
(Fadeout. Music.)

Act I

SCENE 3

A few days later. It's day. Adam is sitting in a corner intently carving a piece of cane with a knife. He is making himself a flute. Angel enters, greeting invisible animals that are passing by.

ANGEL: Hello, Mrs. Hen, how are those eggs coming along? I'll drop by for the big event. Hello, Mr. Ram, how's your missus? Give her my regards, and tell her I hope she produces the finest set of lambs in the garden. Hello, Mrs. Fly, when's the big day? I can't wait to see a whole cloud of little flies zooming around. Oh, what a lovely day!

ADAM: I'm glad to see you're in such good spirits.

ANGEL: Things are moving right along, my friend Adam. They're certain to be very pleased with my work up there. They'll probably promote me to a higher order.

ADAM: Congratulations.

ANGEL: That's a bit premature. At the beginning one is new on the job, and it all seems quite overwhelming. . . . But the machine has been set in motion. It's all beginning to boil. The trees are sending out new shoots, the animals are multiplying, the plants are blooming. . . .

ADAM: Wonderful for you.

ANGEL: You look a little depressed.

ADAM: No, not really.

ANGEL: And where's Lili?

ADAM: Out there, with the horses. She adores horses.

ANGEL: Have you two had another fight?

ADAM: I don't want to talk about it.

ANGEL: Adam, I don't mean to meddle in your affairs, but I think you should make a greater effort. Lili's a splendid person.

ADAM: Don't you realize she's determined to have everything her way?

ANGEL: So? What about you?

ADAM: One of us has to be the one to give orders.

ANGEL: Why?

ADAM: Because in this world somebody always has to be in charge. The Lord has set us an example. He gives the orders, and everything runs smoothly.

ANGEL: But you aren't the Lord.

ADAM: I'm certain He wants it that way.

ANGEL: If you hadn't torn up those books, we could have found out what He wanted.

ADAM: You want to know why I tore them up? Because her insolence drove me to it.

ANGEL: Shall I tell you why you really destroyed them? Because you didn't like in the slightest what was written in them.

ADAM: Go take a walk.

ANGEL: What are you making?

ADAM: A flute. You blow through the end, and sounds come out through the holes, like birdsongs. I'm going to leave the end open. Women don't know how to invent. They aren't clever with their hands.

ANGEL: By the way, there's a matter that's been bothering me.... Up there what interests them most is you ... the humans. So it's best that things progress according to plan. But if you don't progress, they can make it difficult for me. Do you follow? There's a lot of jealousy and rivalry in the service. In other words, for the good of us all, I'd like you to augment your family right away. I suppose there's ... nothing yet?

ADAM: Nothing what? What do you mean?

ANGEL: *(Imitating pregnancy with his hands.)* You know ...

ADAM: Oh, no ... nothing like that.

ANGEL: But you and she ... don't you? *(Trying to convey the idea of intercourse with his hands.)*

ADAM: You mean do she and I? ... Oh, sure, all the time.

ANGEL: Then, why not? *(Imitating pregnancy once again.)*

ADAM: Ask her.

ANGEL: What's wrong? Is it that she doesn't like to ...

ADAM: Lili? Better than eating. So do I. On that point there's no argument. It's very beneficial exercise. Haven't you ever tried it?

ANGEL: Aren't you forgetting who I am?

ADAM: Oh, I'm sorry. But you don't know what you're missing. *(Returning to the flute.)* Let's see how this works. *(He blows, and some timid notes come out.)* Did you hear that? I've just composed. I'm a musician, Angel. A musician! *(He plays again.)*

ANGEL: *(Applauding.)* Bravo.

ADAM: *(Taking a bow like a real artist.)* Thank you, thank you. Are you convinced now that I'm the superior one?

(The same music is heard from offstage.)

ADAM: What was that?

ANGEL: It must have been the echo.

ADAM: But of course. The echo.

(The sound of hoofbeats; then Lili enters, skipping and dancing and playing her flute like a virtuoso.)

LILI: *(Happy.)* Did you hear it? I've just composed a melody. I'm a musician, Angel. A musician!

ADAM: Where did you get that flute?

LILI: I made it. But I see you have one, too. They're wonderful.

ADAM: Lili, give me your flute!

LILI: Why do you want it?

ADAM: In this Paradise I will not tolerate any flute except mine.

LILI: We can play them together, silly. It will sound delightful.

ADAM: Where have you ever seen a woman playing music? *(He grabs her flute.)*

LILI: Don't do that, Adam, or you'll regret it the rest of your life.

ADAM: I'll do what I please. *(He breaks her flute.)*

LILI: *(Tearful.)* No! Oh, no! Why did you do that? You . . . beast! Did you see, Angel?

ANGEL: Of course I saw it, Lili. An act of savagery.

LILI: And I was feeling so happy with my music.

ANGEL: *(To Lili.)* When you have a few children running around, all this will change. You'll see. Wouldn't you like to have children?

LILI: I suppose I would.

ANGEL: Then cheer up, and full speed ahead. Let's see if you can finally hit the jackpot.

LILI: It's not so simple.

ADAM: Why not? Plum, plum . . . and let nature take its course.

LILI: A child is too important to bring into the world just any old way.

ADAM: *(To Angel.)* Do you know what she does? She takes a bath after making love so not a trace remains on her.

ANGEL: *(To Lili.)* Why do you do that, foolish girl?

LILI: Because my body is involved, and I'm the one who has to decide, not him. As soon as he pulls up his zipper, you'll see him nosing around out there somewhere while I'll spend nine months carrying the bundle.

ANGEL: Perhaps if you shared the work. You carry the bundle one time, and he does it the next.

ADAM: Me? You're out of your mind!

LILI: To tell the truth, I wouldn't renounce having any of my children for anything in this world. Even knowing that it ends in an ordeal they call childbirth.

ADAM: Tell me about it.

LILI: It's better not to tell you. Your hair would stand on end. But when the baby arrives, I won't let him do with it what he did to the flute.

ADAM: Remind her that I'm her husband and that what's here is mine. *(To Lili.)* Flute, children, and property rights. I'm the seed; you're only the flowerpot.

LILI: *(To Angel.)* Listen to him!

ANGEL: *(To Lili.)* It's only a figure of speech. . . . *(To Adam.)* Enough is enough, idiot.

LILI: What interest does he have in the matter? With him it's "I want it now, I get it now," and then he's off to who knows where.

ANGEL: But you'll never start multiplying that way.

LILI: And why should he be the only one to run the adding machine?

ADAM: It's impossible to reason with you.

LILI: You still don't get it.

ANGEL: What are you going to do?

LILI: Rather than feel myself so little understood, I prefer to go away and live alone.

ANGEL: What?

LILI: We'll get a divorce.

ANGEL: It would be a catastrophe if you leave, a cataclysm. What would become of the human race?

ADAM: I warn you, you won't find a substitute. Don't you see that I'm the only man in the world?

LILI: And I'm also the only woman.

ANGEL: And you're going off to live alone because of a minor point of etiquette?

LILI: You saw what he did to the flute. I spent the whole morning carving it.

ADAM: Some feat.

LILI: I wouldn't want to end up like the flute.

ANGEL: I can fix that in a jiffy. Come here, give me your flute. *(He takes Adam's flute and gives it to Lili.)* Here, for you. *(To Adam.)* And now, ask her to forgive you. Come on, come on.

ADAM: *(After hesitating.)* Look, Angel, I don't meddle in your affairs, so you let me take care of mine as I see fit.

LILI: Don't go on, Adam. It's over. Fini. I'm leaving.

ADAM: Okay, leave . . . but go to our hut. Then we can talk about it in private.

LILI: No, thank you. I'll never go back there.

ADAM: Do as you please, then. See if I care!

ANGEL: It's downright madness! Please, Adam, get control of yourself!

ADAM: I'll have you know that you're not the only female in this place. There are cows, nanny goats, and even giraffes with less conceit and more character than you.

ANGEL: Have you lost your mind? Oh, my God, I think I'm going to be sick.

LILI: Do you know what's happening, Adam? Do you really know why you want to brand me like a cow? Because here . . . *(Indicating her stomach)* is the future of the human race. Here is the history of the world. And down deep you're envious.

ADAM: You're the one who's envious because my penis is bigger than yours.

LILI: Envious of that ugly thing that hangs on you and frightened you the first time you saw it? Not even you could believe that joke. Goodbye, Adam.

ADAM: Goodbye, Lili. Go. Go to the devil. I never want to see you again.
(Lili exits.)

ANGEL: What have you done?

ADAM: Don't worry. She'll be back.

ANGEL: Stupid. She'll never come back. *(Pause.)* Well, I'll have to leave, too.

ADAM: You?

ANGEL: Surely you understand that if you don't reproduce it's the end of all this.

ADAM: You can leave. Everything can leave. Birds, snakes, fish, trees, moon. . . . Leave me alone!

ANGEL: You are pigheaded! I don't want to think what they'll say to me when I go back up there. . . . *(Pause.)* I've just had a great idea. Why don't you run look for her?

ADAM: What are you up to? Do you want her to wear the pants and order me around for the rest of my life? Never. But I have a better idea. Why don't we ask the Lord to create another woman for us? One that's not so complicated.

ANGEL: Oh, don't even think it. He'd be furious! And you don't know what that's like.

ADAM: But when He finds out there won't be any offspring here . . .

ANGEL: Hush, don't remind me of that.

ADAM: Just between you and me, I don't think it would be very difficult.

ANGEL: And how do you propose we start?

ADAM: You must know how. You were present at creation. A different kind of woman . . . sweet, submissive, sacrificing, a homebody . . . one baby after another . . . not too bright.

ANGEL: And if He found out?

ADAM: He'll be happy when He sees the world full of little men and women who look just like Him. And the reward for your initiative will be even greater . . .

ANGEL: No, I don't dare.

ADAM: What could we call her? Something short and simple that sounds good with Adam. Adam and Ave? Adam and Ove? No. How about Eve? Adam and Eve. Yes, that has a solid ring to it.

ANGEL: It sounds all right. And it's spelled the same backward and forward. . . . What am I saying? No!

ADAM: Hello, Eve. Run to the kitchen, Eve. Get in bed, Eve, I'm ready. Eve, bring me a beer. Eve . . . it doesn't sound bad, does it? Angel, be a friend. Do it as a personal favor. Will you please create Eve for me?

CURTAIN or LIGHTS DOWN

Act II

SCENE 1

Angel and Adam are onstage. Angel has a bag of earth and a bucket of water.

ADAM: What have you got there?

ANGEL: What do you think I've got? Earth from the ravine and water from the lake to mix it with.

ADAM: Oh . . . do you intend to make her out of mud?

ANGEL: How else? That's how the Lord did it.

ADAM: But it didn't turn out all that well for Him. You've already seen the results.

ANGEL: If you keep on criticizing the Lord, I'm going to get mad and you can create your woman all by yourself.

ADAM: It was her attitude. But we should use another material if we want to improve the product.

ANGEL: You can only make clay with earth. And this is the very best quality . . . the same as you were made from.

ADAM: But if she turns out exactly like the other one, we've already got trouble on our hands. She'll want to be equal, too, and she'll freak me out.

ANGEL: You don't want Eve to be like you?

ADAM: More or less, but different.

ANGEL: How exactly?

ADAM: More typical, with long hair and short ideas. Do you understand?

ANGEL: No.

ADAM: With a good body, firm breasts, and a nice pair of legs. She'll know how to stretch out when I'm ready to make love. If she wants to know something, I'll explain it to her. She'll have the perfect life, and she won't have anything to complain about.

ANGEL: We'll see what happens. If only you hadn't destroyed those books.

ADAM: There are a couple left. Look, here's a "Treatise on Surgery," with some wonderful pictures.

ANGEL: For all the good it's going to do us. . . . It'll be centuries before we have an operating room at our disposal.

ADAM: (Handing him another book.) "Childbirth." This is the only part that worries me. Because if she delivers the babies, no matter how submissive she is at the start, sooner or later she may step out of line like the other one.

ANGEL: What do you expect?

ADAM: She'll start with the same drivel. "I'm the mother of your children, without me the species would end . . ."

ANGEL: Isn't that true?

ADAM: That's exactly why it has to be avoided.

ANGEL: How do you propose to do that?

ADAM: Just as I come from the Lord, she must come from me.

ANGEL: Do you think you're God?

ADAM: Well, do you or don't you want to populate the earth?

ANGEL: But . . .

ADAM: Come here. I'll tell you what I have in mind. You'll cut out a tiny piece of my body. A very small piece so it doesn't hurt. Mix it with the clay. I'll leave the artistic part to you. It will always be on record that she has sprung from me. Then she can bear all the children she wishes . . . and who will have been the first, the source of everything? Me.

ANGEL: Do tell. Now I get it. You're a real bastard.

ADAM: And you're a fuddy-duddy, Archangel. . . .

ANGEL: Well, let's give it a try. *(He picks up a pair of scissors and clicks them as he walks around Adam like a sheepshearer.)* Now let's see what we can cut off! It has to be something you don't really need . . . something that hangs loose.

ADAM: *(Putting his hands over his crotch.)* No! Not what you're thinking.

ANGEL: Then tell me what to cut off.

ADAM: If I had a tail, it would be perfect. Maybe something I have more than one of so it won't be so noticeable.

ANGEL: A finger?

ADAM: No. I may decide to take up the flute again. . . . I've got it! A rib. I have a lot of them. Feel.

ANGEL: Oh, no! That's too difficult to get out.

ADAM: The surgery book must have instructions. Wait until I'm sound asleep, and zas! Look, here it is. Page thirty-three. *(He stretches out on the desk and puts the book on top so that Angel can see it.)* Okay?

ANGEL: Okay.

ADAM: A single rib. The smallest, the extra one. And don't hurt. . . .

ANGEL: I'll give it a try. *(He puts on the glasses and reads.)* "Take the scalpel in the right hand, and separate the skin of the sternum with the left . . ." I don't understand any of this. My God, what a ghastly profession.

As he stands there, very worried and bewildered, holding the scissors like a scalpel, the lights fade and loud music is heard. In a moment the lights come up again. It is late afternoon. Angel and Adam are turning a jump rope while Eve jumps up and down like a child. She is like a beautiful doll and is dressed in a short skirt and blouse—both edged with tacky feminine frills.

EVE: *(Skipping and singing.)*

Eve be nimble, Eve be quick,

Eve jumps over the candlestick.

Eve be nimble, Eve be quick,

Eve's the cutest little trick. . . .

ANGEL & ADAM: Very good! Very good!

EVE: *(Clapping.)* Again, again. . . .

ANGEL: Eve, we've spent the whole afternoon turning rope with you. You've done nothing but skip rope since the day you were born.

EVE: I happen to like it very much. Please, pretty please.

ADAM: Run along, Eve, and don't bother Angel. We'll do it again tomorrow.

EVE: Anything you say, Adam. You know better than anyone what I should do.

ADAM: Of course I do. Now give me a kiss.

EVE: With all my heart and soul. *(She kisses his hand with great respect.)* Are you thirsty? Can I bring you some water from the spring? Or do you prefer some fruit?

ADAM: Water.

EVE: I'll be right back. *(She brushes off his T-shirt with her fingers.)* You had some leaves on you. I always want you to be immaculate. *(She throws him a kiss and exits.)*

ANGEL: She didn't turn out bad at all, did she?

ADAM: No, not bad.

ANGEL: Pretty, submissive, dumb ... just like you wanted her. I don't suppose you have any complaints.

ADAM: She's much more feminine than the other one. Really filled out, especially behind. Maybe you used a little too much clay.

ANGEL: You don't like that?

ADAM: She's so sweet, so obedient. . . . You saw how she kissed me when I asked her to. She jumps when I say jump. *(Snapping his fingers.)* Hey, you, little girl ... no sooner said than done. That's domestic bliss for you.

ANGEL: Of course ...

ADAM: *(Shouting.)* I'm delighted with Eve. She's my ideal. Do you hear? Delighted!

ANGEL: How can I help hearing if you shout like that!
    (Pause.)

ADAM: Where do you suppose she is?

ANGEL: She went to get water for you.

ADAM: I meant Lili.

ANGEL: Oh, I don't know ... roundabout.

ADAM: I hope nothing has happened to her.

ANGEL: Don't worry. She's very clever.

ADAM: That's her worst defect. I don't like clever women, especially when they keep reminding you how smart they are. I can't stand Lili! Do you understand?

ANGEL: I understand. Oh, yes.

ADAM: Don't think I miss her. It would be natural, of course, if I did . . . after all, she was my first wife. Don't tell me it wouldn't be natural to miss her!

ANGEL: No, I won't tell you that.

ADAM: As pigheaded as she is . . . it wouldn't surprise me if she turned up unexpectedly. What do you think?

ANGEL: How would I know?

ADAM: Let her! Hello, Lili; hello, Adam, and that's it. Would you like for her to come back sometime?

ANGEL: Well . . .

ADAM: Just to see her. There's nothing wrong in seeing a person. . . .

ANGEL: No, actually no. But . . .

ADAM: Lili's probably just the way she was. I don't deny that, but I have to recognize one thing, my friend, she had a very special way of making love . . . a very personal way!

ANGEL: Enough! Stop where you are. I won't put up with it!

ADAM: But what did I say wrong?

ANGEL: Eve is your wife, Adam.

ADAM: Of course she is.

ANGEL: Made to order, like a suit.

ADAM: Most assuredly. What are you driving at?

ANGEL: Look, I'll be as naive and as angelical as you wish, and I'll try to please you . . . but don't expect me to be a confidant for your erotic fantasies. Never! Understand? Never!

ADAM: Stop! You are offending my wife, Eve.

ANGEL: *I'm* offending her?

ADAM: I will not allow you to besmirch the name of that saintly woman.

ANGEL: Can I say something . . . ?

ADAM: There is not and there will never be any woman for me except Eve. Never forget that!

ANGEL: I won't. I swear. I hope you'll do the same.
(Eve enters with a lamb in her arms.)

EVE: Look, Adam, what a darling little lamb. Isn't he the sweetest itsy-bitsy thing you've ever seen?

ADAM: Itsy-bitsy! Ugh. What a stupid expression!

EVE: I'll never say it again if you don't like it. Forgive me.

ADAM: What about my water?

EVE: Oh, I forgot. I saw the sheep's little darlings, and I'm simply crazy about children.

ADAM: You're a hopeless case. You put pleasure before your husband's needs. I should give you something to remember!

EVE: I'll go get it right now.

ADAM: I'll go. I don't trust you. My wife is so useless she doesn't even know how to bring me a drink of water.

EVE: No, please let me go . . .

ADAM: It's too late. I forbid you in the future to waste your time gossiping with your women friends and neglecting your family duties. *(He exits in a huff.)*

EVE: He has every right to be angry with me. I'm a bad wife. I feel guilty.

ANGEL: My dear, he'll get over it.

EVE: He's so good! *(Transition.)* Do you know how many babies the sheep had? Seven. I'd like to have seven, too, all at once, like the sheep.

ANGEL: One right after the other . . . ?

EVE: I want a baby, Angel, a baby like this one. He's a darling, isn't he?

ANGEL: First you have to take the bull by the horns.

EVE: What are you talking about?

ANGEL: You don't know anything, do you?

EVE: I? About what?

ANGEL: Maybe I should relate a few things to you so it won't come as a complete surprise.

EVE: Are you going to tell me a story? I adore fairy tales.

ANGEL: How am I going to go about this? Butterflies, for example. The boy butterfly flies around the girl butterfly . . . he kisses her . . .

EVE: *(Clapping.)* And little butterflies are born.

ANGEL: Correct.

EVE: Oh, you almost had me worried. I've also kissed Adam. On the hand.

ANGEL: That's not bad for a start.

EVE: It's not enough?

ANGEL: No, my dear, it's not enough. *(He explodes.)* That an Archangel of my rank should have to take charge of this is too much!

EVE: I don't understand.

ANGEL: Well, to put it bluntly . . . you just lie still, without moving, and let Adam do all the rest, whatever it may be.

EVE: You frighten me.

ANGEL: Just think of something else while it's happening. Courage, my dear. Everything has its price.
(Adam enters.)

ADAM: Are you two still talking? More gossip?

ANGEL: I was explaining a few things to her. Since it's your wedding night, your honeymoon . . . I was thinking . . . why not take her somewhere on a wedding trip?

EVE: Why go to all that bother? Some other time, maybe . . .

ADAM: Well, it's not a bad idea. . . . *(He gives her a pat on the buttocks.)* What do you say, doll?

EVE: No, no, no . . .

ADAM: What's wrong with you?

EVE: I don't know. I'm afraid.

ADAM: Don't be silly.

ANGEL: *(Taking the lamb from her.)* Wait. *(He puts a wedding veil on Eve's head.)* You look lovely. Now for a little rice. *(He throws it.)* Congratulations. May you live happily ever after. And be prolific. What would the newspapers say of a historic event like this? *(To Adam.)* Go on, now, take her in your arms and carry her to the bridal suite. Tum-tum-tum-tum. Tum-tum-tum-tum . . .

(As Adam starts to exit with Eve in his arms, he hears the "Wedding March" from offstage played on a flute, and he stops in his tracks.)

ADAM: Did you hear that, Angel?

ANGEL: I'm not deaf.

EVE: What a pretty sound. That's not a bird.

ANGEL: No, Eve, it's not a bird.

EVE: Then what is it? What's it called?

ADAM: It's called a flute. But if somebody thinks she's going to spoil my wedding night, she's very mistaken. So? Have you satisfied your curiosity? Then let's go.

(They exit.)

ANGEL: At last. And you, Lili, would you stop playing that damn flute! Stop it! *(Suddenly he exits, running.)* I'll fix her! I'll kill her!

(The sound of the flute goes sour after a few moments and stops. Then we hear the hoofbeats of a horse galloping away. Light change. Day. Lili is seated on a limb of the Tree of Good and Evil, her legs dangling as she eats an apple. Shortly afterward Adam enters, very bored. He is carrying a golf club and an orange. He places the orange on the ground and is about to hit it with the club when he sees Lili.)

ADAM: Lili! What are you doing here?

LILI: Eating an apple, as you can see. These are the biggest and tastiest in all of Paradise. Want a bite?

ADAM: You know I don't like them.

LILI: I forgot. By the way, how's your marriage going?

ADAM: Very well. I'm very happy, and we're going to have a child. Many children. Flocks of children.

LILI: I'm glad for you.

ADAM: Thank you. And you? How's your life?

LILI: Just fine.

ADAM: I'm glad.

LILI: I go horseback riding. I've learned a lot about horses. I tame them, I watch them graze . . . and a thousand other things.

ADAM: You don't get bored?

LILI: I should say not! Since our separation I haven't been bored for a minute. I also study music.

ADAM: I realized that on my wedding night.

LILI: It didn't take you long to find a substitute for me. . . .

ADAM: Well, what did you expect? That I was going to live alone and mope around the rest of my days? The race has to reproduce itself. I'm in favor of progress, technology, and self-development.

LILI: But of course. (Transition.) Hello, Adam.

ADAM: Hello, Lili. And goodbye.

LILI: You're leaving?

ADAM: I'm not. You are! Eve could turn up any moment. . . .

LILI: I'm a free woman. I can be where I like.

ADAM: It would be awful if she saw you.

LILI: Why? Oh, I get it. She doesn't know I exist. You still haven't had the courage to tell her that she's your second wife and that she's married to a divorced man. Adam, sometimes you trouble me.

ADAM: Are you starting again? You've interfered with my life enough, don't you think?

LILI: I was only interested in your welfare. . . . I also feel sorry for that poor girl.

ADAM: *(Transition.)* You know, you're very pretty today.

LILI: Thank you.

ADAM: Eve's very pretty, too, of course.

LILI: Of course.

ADAM: We had a good life, you and I, didn't we?

LILI: Well, sometimes.

ADAM: Oh, but I have a sensational life with Eve, too.

LILI: Of course.

ADAM: We were a lucky couple. We invented the kiss, love, reconciliation.

LILI: But you were determined to destroy it all. . . . What's the game you're playing? *(Referring to the golf club and the orange.)*

ADAM: Just a stupid thing I thought up to kill time. Even though I don't really need to . . . because I have such an exciting life.

LILI: I'm sure you do.

ADAM: Lili . . . since you left I've been bored silly. I don't do anything except take walks. My feet are killing me from so much walking.

LILI: But what about your wife?

ADAM: The poor thing doesn't know how to talk about anything. She only likes to skip rope and pet the babies of all the animals. . . . Making love with her is like making love alone!

LILI: Don't go on. I don't want to hear about it.

ADAM: When I think of the notes you took for us. . . . Look, I still have them.

LILI: I don't want to see them. *(She picks another apple and takes a bite.)*

ADAM: What do you suppose they call what we're feeling at this moment? It's the first time.

LILI: It's always the first time.

ADAM: We'll have to find a name for it.

LILI: Nostalgia, longing, sadness . . . I don't know. You can choose.

ADAM: Maybe it's one that's already been invented . . . love.

(He takes the apple from her hand and throws it on the ground. They kiss. Angel surprises them.)

ANGEL: Oh, no! I forbid it! Shameless, indecent . . . adulterers!

ADAM: Adulterers no.

ANGEL: But Adam, she's your neighbor's wife!

ADAM: What neighbor?

ANGEL: Look, don't get me confused. You know very well what I mean. And this is dreadful!

ADAM: But Angel . . .

ANGEL: Don't Angel me! What kind of a Paradise is this going to be if everyone goes around kissing whomever he pleases!

LILI: I am a liberated woman, and I'll do what I damn please, whether you like it or not. Arrivederci. Ciao. *(She exits.)*

ANGEL: And you! What a disgrace! With a sweet wife and mother-to-be all in one waiting for you at home. . . . Didn't I make her exactly the way you asked me to, with a little piece of rib and all? Well, you have the obligation to love her, by force if necessary.

ADAM: Oh, I love her, too.

ANGEL: What?

ADAM: Actually, I want them both. One to take care of the house and one to take care of me. . . .

ANGEL: And who do you take care of? You're a hypocrite. I don't know why I talk to you.

(Eve enters. She is wearing an apron and is going around dusting the leaves with a little feather duster.)

EVE: *(Humming.)* "Eve be nimble, Eve be quick, etc." Paradise will be sparkling when I get through with it. Not a speck of dust or a branch out of place. I'm the genuine article: a homemaker, with my little garden and my baby. *(She touches her stomach.)* I'm the happiest woman in the world.

ADAM: I'm going for a walk.

EVE: Again?

ADAM: I'll work up an appetite for dinner.

EVE: Today I'm serving lettuce, radishes, plums, and melons, just as you like them. And a surprise for dessert!

ADAM: Fine.

EVE: Adam, you don't love me the way you used to.

ADAM: Why do you talk such nonsense?

EVE: You haven't asked me what the surprise is.

ADAM: If you tell me, it won't be a surprise any longer. Besides, I know what it is: bananas.

EVE: How did you ever guess?

ADAM: Because you give me bananas for dessert every day. And I'm fed up with bananas! I'll see you later. *(He starts off in the direction Lili took.)*

ANGEL: *(Pointing in the opposite direction.)* That way.

ADAM: What do you mean?

ANGEL: You can take all the walks you want, but in that direction. Do we understand each other? I'd better go with you, just in case.

(They exit together.)

EVE: *(Speaking to her stomach.)* How are you getting along, little one? Your father's going to become the champion long-distance walker. *(She goes on cleaning and humming her song. She picks up something from the ground: the partially eaten apple. She goes on humming as she looks at it attentively.)* Heaven help me, it's an apple from the forbidden tree! And someone has taken a bite! Adam, what have you done?!! *(She looks closer.)* But this isn't Adam's bite. He has a much bigger mouth. . . . But if Adam didn't, who did? Since Angel is a pure spirit, he doesn't eat or drink. . . . Oh, what am I thinking? Why, it has lipstick marks! There's another woman in this garden! *(Having an attack of hysteria.)* Aaaeeee!

(Adam and Angel enter, running.)

ADAM: What's wrong with you?

EVE: Don't come close. Don't you touch me.

ADAM: But Eve . . .

EVE: Look. *(She gives the apple to Adam.)*

ADAM: Of all things. *(He passes it to Angel.)*

ANGEL: You took the words right out of my mouth: of all things.

EVE: And that is lipstick. I'm a deceived wife, Angel. I'm the first deceived wife of the human race! Aaaaaeeeee!

ADAM: Don't shriek like that, for God's sake.

EVE: I feel awful, and I want to die. If it weren't for the innocent child I'm carrying inside me, I'd throw myself under a train this very minute. Aaaaeeee!

ADAM: What train? If you don't shut up I'll give you something to cry about.

EVE: Would you be capable of striking me in my condition?

ANGEL: He'd be capable. You'd better close your mouth. Believe me.

EVE: Well, if he hits me I'm leaving him.

ANGEL: Now this little hypocrite wants to leave. It's getting to be an epidemic. And just where would you go, dear girl?

EVE: Where any respectable woman goes: home to mother.

ADAM: Eve . . . A man is a man and a woman is a woman. And some things have to be done by men and other things by women. Do you agree?

EVE: Yes, but how do you explain the apple?

ADAM: What apple? Oh, you mean the . . . Why, it has a very simple explanation . . . quite simple. . . . Go on, you explain it, Angel, and she'll be satisfied.

ANGEL: I'm sure you can do it much better than I.

ADAM: You flatter me.

ANGEL: I'm eager to hear an explanation myself.

ADAM: *(Suddenly furious.)* I don't have to give an explanation to anybody! You get that? And if you took care of your family the way you're supposed to, you wouldn't be concerned with apples. Besides, it's lunchtime, and you know I like to have my meals punctually.

EVE: Oh, I'm so unhappy!

ADAM: To offend me this way with your unfounded suspicions. Me, who made you a mother. And there's nothing greater than motherhood. I've always been against divorce, abortion, premarital relations, and all the other liberties that threaten the sanctity of family. A family that prays together stays together!

EVE: That's all fine and good, but who is the woman who eats apples?

ADAM: *(To Angel.)* See? It's impossible to reason with her.

ANGEL: But Adam . . .

ADAM: *(Superior.)* You're right, my friend. It's best to keep calm. *(He looks at his watch.)* Let's get ready to eat in our home sweet home. *(Offering Eve his arm.)* Eve . . .
(Eve takes Adam's arm and Angel's on the other side. Pretending everything is fine, they sing Eve's song and dance to the music.)

ADAM & ANGEL:
"Eve is nimble, Eve is quick,
Eve's the cutest little trick. . . . etc."

EVE: *(Pulling free.)* You're birds of a feather. But I'll find out, you rascals, I will! *(She exits, running.)*

ADAM: Eve!

ANGEL: Eve! . . . Oh, my goodness!
(They follow her offstage.)
(Blackout and music.)

Act II

SCENE 2

When the lights come up, Lili is seated in the apple tree reading a book and eating an apple. Eve appears. Her pregnancy is quite advanced. She goes toward the tree with a certain air of mystery, looking on the ground for an apple core. Lili absentmindedly tosses away her apple and it falls near Eve, who looks up and sees Lili.

EVE: Aha, I've finally found you. I knew you'd come back sooner or later for your apples.

LILI: Hello, Eve.

EVE: Who are you? Where did you come from? What are you up to?

LILI: Get off your high horse, dear. I was here long before you. I am, how shall I say, your predecessor.

EVE: That's a lie. Adam would have told me.

LILI: Since when do men tell their wives the story of their life?

EVE: I shouldn't even be talking to you.

LILI: Of course not. You should avoid me like the plague. Danger zone: no admission without protective clothing. I'm free, and I think for myself. That spells danger!

EVE: And nothing happens to you when you eat the apples?

LILI: See for yourself. I'm alone. When someone doesn't surrender unconditionally, they separate them from society, put them in isolation. I'll bet they just love you, don't they?

EVE: They say I'm adorable.

LILI: But heaven help you if you step out of character and disobey.

EVE: I'm going to have a baby. He's in here, you know. *(She caresses her stomach.)*

LILI: Can you feel it move?

EVE: He kicks sometimes.

LILI: Can I feel? Don't worry, I'm not going to hurt it. *(She has come down from the tree and touches Eve's stomach.)* How nice. . . . This is what really irks me . . . that they want to use this child as a subtle trap to enslave you.

EVE: That's not true. He'll be mine. All mine. . . .

LILI: He'll be Adam's, he'll carry his name. They'll see to it that he works for Adam, and they'll send him off to war. You'll only have served to give birth.

EVE: What's your name?

LILI: What does my name matter? I rather like you, Eve. My name's Lili, dangerous Lili, history's bad girl. We should be friends.

EVE: I don't think so.

LILI: Here. I'll give you my book and flute.

EVE: Thanks, but I don't have time for them.

LILI: Do you want to go horseback riding?

EVE: Adam doesn't like for me to go out. *(After a pause.)* Are you my husband's lover?

LILI: I was his wife in another time. . . . We separated before you came on the scene.

EVE: And you made love . . . and all that, naturally.

LILI: Naturally.

EVE: Then . . . have you continued to see him?

LILI: Well, not enough to speak of. . . .

EVE: And do you still make love?

LILI: Much less frequently than he'd like, of course.

EVE: Hand me an apple.

LILI: Why?

EVE: I'm going to eat it right now. I'm going to eat the whole tree. I want to teach that bastard a lesson.

LILI: No, Eve, not just to get even.

EVE: Well, things are going to be different from now on, I can assure you.

LILI: I don't doubt it.

EVE: And as for you with your big-sister attitudes. You're as big a hypocrite as he is, sleeping with the first man who comes along. . . . You, you . . . Jezebel! You're just frustrated and jealous!

LILI: Do you feel better now that you've insulted me?

EVE: Much better, thank you.

LILI: Then we can be friends now?

EVE: Me . . . your friend? How can you even think such a thing? I'm a respectable woman.

LILI: You call this respectability?

EVE: Oh, how I hate you.

LILI: *(Consoling her.)* My poor little Eve.

EVE: Lili, I'm so unhappy! So unhappy!
(They embrace tearfully. Adam enters.)

ADAM: Hey, what's going on?

EVE: Adam, I'd like you to meet my best friend, Lili. Actually, she's my only friend. Silly me, you two already know each other.

ADAM: Everybody knows everybody here.

EVE: I've invited her to dinner. Don't you think that's a wonderful idea?

ADAM: Lili may have other plans. . . .

EVE: I'm sure she'll cancel them just to have dinner in our happy little home.

ADAM: But I wouldn't want to inconvenience her. Some other time, perhaps. . . .

EVE: Lili will be delighted.

ADAM: But I don't . . .

EVE: But you don't what . . . ?

LILI: Will you stop acting like idiots?

ADAM: Lili, why is she behaving this way?

LILI: I've told her everything, from A to Z.

ADAM: How could you do such a thing!

LILI: Now that we all know where we stand, if the invitation still holds, I accept.

EVE: Why don't we eat right here? It's a lovely spot. We'll just have ourselves a little picnic.

LILI: I'll help you.

EVE: Don't bother. I'll go get everything.

ADAM: Eve, I want to explain . . .

EVE: Please, Adam, we have company. We'll talk later. Offer her a drink. We have some marvelous crushed grapes. *(She exits.)*

ADAM: Have you lost your mind?

LILI: I have nothing to hide.

ADAM: *(He offers her a glass.)* You can see how she is. I didn't exaggerate. She's dumb, boring, and irremediably middle-class. But I can't leave her right now. She's pregnant, she's been hurt, and I feel sorry for her. . . .

LILI: If you say another word, I'll break this glass over your head.
   (Pause.)

ADAM: Will you meet me in the usual place?

LILI: I don't think so.

ADAM: Dearest, if you only knew how much I want you.

LILI: Can't you see how things are? I doubt that I'll ever be wanting you again, ever. You swine!

(Eve enters with a tray full of succulent dishes.)

EVE: Dinner's served. You sit right there, Lili.

LILI: All right.

(The three of them sit on the ground around the tray.)

ADAM: Lord, bless this food we are about to eat, and free us from sin. Amen.

EVE: Amen.

LILI: How appetizing it all looks. There's nothing like home-cooked food. Cheers!

ANGEL: *(Entering.)* What's going on!! What does this mean?

LILI: It's called civilization, Angel. We've just invented our marvelous civilization. To your health! *(She drinks.)*

ANGEL: Cut it out! I'm going to telephone the Lord right now to come down and take charge personally. We'll see if He can keep order. It's all very posh for Him up there, taking it easy, without a care in the world, sunbathing, sipping His martinis . . . I can't go on. I've had it. *(He dials a number on the telephone.)* Hello, this is Angel in Extracelestial Services. Connect me with the Lord. It's urgent. I need to speak to Him immediately. I don't care where He is. What? What's that? I've got Limbo? Then this isn't . . . I'm so sorry, I must have dialed the wrong number. *(Hangs up.)* They've driven me bonkers. *(He starts to dial again.)*

LILI: Don't bother to call again, Angel. I'm going.

ANGEL: What?

LILI: This time I'm leaving Paradise. I don't want to see anyone ever.

ADAM: Where will you go?

LILI: I'll get on my horse, and we'll go off and explore the valleys and prairies, splash in the ocean . . . or maybe get lost somewhere out there in the stars.

ANGEL: If you leave this safe haven, you're going to perish!

LILI: We'll risk it. . . . Goodbye, Angel, it's been nice knowing you.

ANGEL: You're going to get me into trouble.

LILI: No more than you're already in. Goodbye, Eve, and don't forget: no matter what they tell you, you're a human being. Goodbye, Adam.

ADAM: Please don't go.

LILI: Take good care of her. And above all, respect her. Even though you force her to stay with you . . . she'll really be as far away from you as I'll be.

ANGEL: You're crying.

LILI: Of course I'm crying. Do you think I'm made of stone? I'm crying because I'm disappointed, I'm sad, I'm angry . . . and above all because I'm disgusted. *(She exits, running. The others stand watching her. There is the sound of hoofbeats, which gradually fades away in the distance.)*

ADAM: I'm leaving Paradise, too.

ANGEL: *(Furious.)* No one is moving from this spot.

ADAM: But Angel . . .

ANGEL: Archangel, if you don't mind. From now on the law is going to be enforced to the letter, without any ifs or buts. Obviously, a firm hand is required. And mine is going to be very firm.

ADAM: All right. And what is the penalty for eating apples from the forbidden tree?

ANGEL: Exile.

ADAM: Eve, bring me an apple immediately. The biggest one.

ANGEL: What are you going to do?

ADAM: Eat it!

EVE: So that you can follow her! Are you planning to abandon me here, alone, homeless, pregnant? You're not going to get rid of me so easily. I can bite, too. Ahmmm! *(She takes a bite with a great show and hands the apple to Adam, who takes a bite in turn. They chomp like two rabbits.)*

ANGEL: They're utterly daffy. This can't be for real. I must be dreaming.

ADAM: *(Spitting noisily.)* Uuufff! It's too sour! I don't like apples at all.

ANGEL: You'd gamble away eternity for one bite . . . and you don't even like apples. It's the last straw!

ADAM: We're at your disposal. Carry out your duty, Archangel.

ANGEL: But . . . *(After a moment of doubt, with a veritable shout he points toward the exit.)* Out!!!!

Act II

SCENE 3

Music and blackout, followed by lightning and thunder. When the lights come up, it's moving day. Packages, books, the desk, and the other equipment are packed and tied. The telephone is on the ground. It is a cold, gray afternoon. Angel is stacking his belongings. Eve enters. She is wearing a shawl over her customary attire.

EVE: Do you have any string?

ANGEL: Here are some short pieces. Take what you want.

EVE: You wouldn't happen to have an extra bag, would you?

ANGEL: No, I'm sorry. Everything's already packed.

EVE: I want to take along some peaches, tomatoes, and a few bananas. . . . I'm frightened, Angel. It's cold for the first time, and there's going to be a storm. What's out there? What fate awaits us and our children?

ANGEL: I don't know. I've never been beyond the stockade that surrounds the garden. At a glance it seems very big. It won't be like this, of course. Why did you do it? You ought to have been more independent and let him eat by himself.

EVE: And what would have become of me without a man? I need him. When all is said and done, I'm only one of his ribs that's come up in the world.

ANGEL: Eve, if you'll give me your word not to tell anyone, I'll let you in on a little secret. But it must stay between you and me.

EVE: Cross my heart.

ANGEL: I didn't take the rib from Adam.

EVE: What?

ANGEL: Oh, I tried to, I assure you, but I couldn't. That book on surgery is written in a gibberish nobody can understand. I'm an Archangel, not Doctor Debakey!

EVE: I don't believe you.

ANGEL: If X-rays are ever invented, you'll be able to confirm it for yourself. Count the ribs, and you'll see that there's the same number on both sides. If I'd taken one out, one would be missing.

EVE: Then . . .

ANGEL: You're made from the same clay. Only clay. Like all human beings whatever their race, their sex, or the color of their skin.

EVE: Why don't you tell him?

ANGEL: I don't dare! It would upset him terribly, with the temper he has. . . . Besides, at this point it wouldn't serve any purpose.
(Adam enters. He is wearing a muffler.)

ADAM: *(Taking two pieces of paper from his pocket.)* This is a list of all we're taking with us.

ANGEL: Bah!

ADAM: *(To Eve.)* Give it to him. And have him sign the duplicate for me. There're not going to be any claims on us after we've gone.

EVE: *(Giving the papers to Angel.)* Here.
(Angel keeps one piece of paper, signs the other and returns it. Adam checks the signature and puts the paper in his pocket.)

ANGEL: *(Putting numbers in the ledger.)* It could be worse. At least the books balance. Account closed. *(He closes the book and puts it away.)* Ready?

ADAM: There's one thing you've forgotten.

ANGEL: What?

ADAM: The Diary. The minutes of what went on. Don't you have to give a detailed account of all that happened here during your administration?

ANGEL: Well, I hadn't gotten around to that. Yes. The official record book, with how it all began, is in the Lord's own handwriting. Now I have to add the other details. *(Scared.)* Oh, this won't be easy.

ADAM: Don't worry. I'll help you remember everything.

ANGEL: I don't need your help.

ADAM: Run along, Eve, go finish packing. I said leave!

EVE: I prefer to stay. I want to know what you write in that book. People are going to read it.

ADAM: What do you think we're going to write? The truth, only the truth. He's an Archangel.

EVE: What about Lili? What are you going to say about her?

ANGEL: *(Reading the book with his glasses on, as always.)* She's not mentioned here by name. The Lord only wrote that He created you male and female.

ADAM: We're male and female, aren't we? Adam and Eve. Why complicate things with more details? Not a word about her. Go on directly to the business of the rib. And let it be very clear that it was Eve who induced me to eat the apple.

EVE: That's not true. You did it so you could run after that woman who put a spell on you.

ADAM: But you gave it to me.

EVE: Only because you asked me for it!

ADAM: You could have refused.

EVE: That's not fair!

ADAM: Stop interfering. We're in a hurry.

ANGEL: *(Consulting his watch.)* Oh, yes. It's getting late.

EVE: *(Exiting in tears.)* Write what you want, for all it matters to me!

ANGEL: Eve's right. You did it for Lili.

ADAM: Let me finish. Lili, at that moment, was the incarnation of temptation, evil. All that she said could have come, for example, from a snake coiled in the tree.

ANGEL: But who ever heard of a snake talking? No sensible person would ever believe such nonsense. Snakes don't even peep. I refuse to write that.

ADAM: *(Grabbing the book.)* Very well. Then I'll do it.

ANGEL: The Lord's Diary! Give it back immediately. What are they going to say up there if I arrive without the book!

ADAM: You can say you lost it, or it got stolen, or that I took it as a remembrance for my descendants.

ANGEL: You are shameless! *(The telephone rings.)* Hello. Yes, you can pick me up whenever you're ready. Ciao. *(He hangs up.)*
(Eve enters, pushing a small cart full of goods and belongings.)

EVE: It's all ready.

ADAM: Are you sure you haven't forgotten anything? *(He checks the things.)*

ANGEL: Eve, don't hold too many hard feelings toward me.

EVE: Angel . . . *(Throwing herself into his arms.)* I'll miss you.

ANGEL: I'll miss you, too. I'm sorry I won't see your child when he's born. . . . He'll be an adorable little cherub for sure.

EVE: Thank you.

ANGEL: Would you prefer a boy or a girl?

ADAM: It'll be a boy! What else?

ANGEL: What are you going to call him?

EVE: I like Abel. It sounds sweet.

ADAM: Cain! My first son will be named Cain. It's a much more manly name.
    Sounds of hoofbeats and the sweet tones of a flute.

EVE: Don't you hear something?

ADAM: I don't hear anything. There's nothing to hear.

EVE: *(To Angel.)* And you?

ANGEL: I'm not deaf.

ADAM: Let's be on our way.

EVE: As you wish.

ADAM: Good luck, Angel.

ANGEL: Stupid, proud idiot, is this the way you say goodbye to me?

ADAM: *(Turning and embracing him.)* Angel!

ANGEL: You are the most pigheaded, selfish creature I've ever met.

ADAM: I'll miss you, old fellow.

ANGEL: And I you . . . you spoiled brat.

EVE: Shall we close the gate when we leave?

ANGEL: For what? In time the stockade will fall down, and no one will recognize
    the place in the world where once there was Paradise. *(To Adam.)* Help her
    push the cart, Adam. Don't you see she can't manage alone?

EVE: Are you still in love with her?

ADAM: That again? Can't you leave me in peace for a moment?

EVE: You'll have to love me. You have no choice now, you know. You're never
    going to be free of me. Because I am and I'll always be your rib. I promise.

ANGEL: *(Indignant.)* Well, I promise both of you that. . . ! Get a move on you. It's
    very late.
    (They start their exit; now both Adam and Eve are pushing the cart.)

ANGEL: But walk closer to her, boy. At least leave Paradise hand in hand.

(They exit.)

ANGEL: Look at them! They lie to each other flagrantly. They love each other and they detest each other. One minute they're wounding and the next they're offering consolation. Who will ever understand this gang of delinquents! I don't want to hear anything else about them, ever; it's over. Out. Enough is enough. . . . Why haven't they come to pick me up? Damn it! *(He grabs the telephone.)* Hello. Are you going to keep me waiting here for eternity? I've had it with them, with you, even with myself. . . . Really? You say you're organizing a special corps of Guardian Angels. . . . Nothing, only . . . if there's still an opening, I'd like you to put me down as a volunteer. Fine. *(He pulls out the telephone and puts it with the other packages that are to be carried away. A fine but persistent rain begins to fall.)* And now it's starting to rain. That's all I needed. And those poor creatures are out there somewhere. . . . But why should I care if they get soaked? We'll just have to see what happens! *(He hangs a "For Sale" sign on the apple tree. He turns up the collar of his jacket, sits down on his packed belongings, and waits. The rain becomes heavier.)*

CURTAIN *or* LIGHTS DOWN

Rigmaroles
(EL SEÑOR DE LAS PATRAÑAS)

A Renaissance Farce in Two Acts by Jaime Salom

Translated by G. J. Racz

Characters

JUAN TIMONEDA, author and printer

ISABEL, his wife

BATISTA, his younger son

VINCENT, his elder son

ANNA, Isabel's niece

SECRETARY TO THE COURT

PURITY, a prostitute

Act I

Interior of Juan Timoneda's print shop in Valencia, which also serves as a tannery and bookshop. Stage left, immense animal hides hang out to dry for future tanning. Stage right, exaggeratedly large and quaintly complex printing machines rise nearly ceiling-high amid a general clutter of presses, shears, papers, and partially bound books. A small, makeshift platform has been erected center stage for rehearsals of the play to be performed during the forthcoming city festival. Downstage a towering vine arbor stands, presumably to provide shade for the front yard of the house.

Facing the audience with (or without) papers in his hand, Juan recites lines from the close of the play he has just read to his family. Isabel, Vincent, Batista, and Anna are seated behind him on the small platform.

JUAN: For what deters sly womankind,
    To artfulness and scheming bred,
    From faithless acts, when so inclined,
    Against her lord and master's bed?
    A woman's thighs obey no rules
    And know not iron chains or locks.
    Those open gates display the jewels
    She tucks away in her gift box.
    In closing, then, let it be said
    Of all the players in the plot
    That every man hath dipped his bread
    Into the same sweet honeypot.
    What matter that their horns be new?
    Think of the happiness they've gained!
    I bid your graces fond adieu.
    Applaud if you leave entertained.

(He concludes and looks at his family. No one says a word.)

Anna, bring your uncle a glass a water. My gullet is completely dry from all this reading.

(Anna obeys him without speaking.)

ISABEL: Would you like to know what I think, Juan Timoneda?

JUAN: Speak up, woman. Plays are written to provide the audience with pleasure, and you are audience, too, even if you are my wife.

ISABEL: Well, I think you are a PIG!

(She slaps him. Anna has entered with a glass of water, which she hands to her uncle.)

JUAN: And here is what I think, Isabel Ferrandis, about what you think.

(He throws the water in her face. The others surround them.)

ISABEL: You will not perform this filth in my house.

JUAN: Don't be so provincial.

ISABEL: That's what you are.

JUAN: You're a stupid woman.

BATISTA: For heaven's sake, father.

ISABEL: Here in Spain, may the Virgin bless us, women have never been improper, and we will not tolerate malicious attacks on our virtue.

JUAN: Even the Court Secretary to Her Highness the Vicereine has complimented me on the play.

ISABEL: Her Highness the Vicereine is an indecent person, and so are you. And she's a foreigner to boot.

JUAN: Christ almighty, Isabel! Do you hear what you're saying?

ISABEL: All she's good for is to sit around eating and laughing the day away, as if not a soul were starving or going into debt to pay her tributes. I don't know how His Highness the Patriarch, who is a saint, can consent to such things.

JUAN: That's enough! You're an uneducated illiterate who knows nothing about the fashions coming to us from the rest of the world.

ISABEL: What do you mean, "world"? You've never set foot from Valencia.

JUAN: Oh, and Valencia is not part of the world?

ISABEL: Not that world, thank God.

JUAN: What would you know about Petrarch or Boccaccio?

ISABEL: I'm not acquainted with your drinking buddies.

JUAN: My God, what a woman! Where ever did I pluck her from?

ISABEL: The river, don't you remember? From the river, when I was training to be a laundress and you would come to fetch buckets of water to tan those hides. And maybe even to peek at my calves when I'd bend over. You've been out for mischief all your life, Juan.

JUAN: Who, me? I wasn't the only one combing the riverbank to see a little skin. The higher you could stretch and make your skirt rise in the back, the better, eh?

ISABEL: That's a lie!

JUAN: Oh, is it? Well, what about that mendicant friar from St. Eustace's monastery, the one who slobbered all over himself whenever you'd hang a sheet and your bodice would open?

ISABEL: He said I reminded him of Veronica, who comforted Christ in His passion.

JUAN: I know full well what that swine was passionate about.

ISABEL: You musn't talk that way in front of the children.

JUAN: That old codger, in hot pursuit of your bottom instead of evildoers.

ISABEL: That's enough.

JUAN: And you, using every trick in the book to make sure he'd never lose sight of it.

ISABEL: You stop right there, Juan Timoneda. When it comes to virtue, no woman can boast of more than my mother's daughter. You know full well that no one but you has ever stormed this fort, and then only after benefit of clergy.

VINCENT: Don't get all riled, mother.

ISABEL: It's one thing to engage in a little coyness at that age and even some touching or heavy petting or some such chaste amusements of youth—after all, we're sensible people, we don't take merchandise home without examining it—but it's quite another thing to lower the drawbridge and surrender the castle to the first besieger who comes along. Much less when it happens over and over again, like in that lewd rigmarole you insist on performing in our house. . . .

ANNA: What can I say? I thought it was a fine play. I mean, if three men can give a woman pleasure at the same time, why should she deprive herself of any of them?

ISABEL: Do you hear your niece, Juan Timoneda?

ANNA: Every woman should do as she pleases with her virginity. It's hers and hers alone for good reason.

ISABEL: You're mistaken, Anna. A proper maiden's hymen belongs to her parents, relatives, brothers, sisters, neighbors, even all of Valencia!

JUAN: Kind of like the public works.

ANNA: For goodness sake, auntie, we aren't in the Middle Ages any more. The Renaissance began years ago. Man's rebirth!

ISABEL: What? Who's giving birth? Good God, don't scare me like that.

JUAN: It's not what you're thinking, Isabel.

ISABEL: But now you've put the buzz in my ear. I want to check this instant—do you hear me?—this very instant to make sure you're still intact.

ANNA: As if I'd let you!

ISABEL: Oh, how disrespectful! See what you achieve with those dirty plays you write?

(She cries.)

BATISTA: Don't cry, mother.

VINCENT: Come on, the poor girl never leaves the house except to go to Mass with you.

ISABEL: Though she'd just love to run through the streets and plazas from dawn to dusk, like some processional banner.

ANNA: Who wouldn't? Trapped inside these four walls day and night. . . .

ISABEL: And you'll stay that way until you marry a gentleman and start a family that will bring credit to us all.

JUAN: Your aunt only wants what's best for you, child. Our family comes from humble stock, but thanks to the kindness of Our Lady the Vicereine, who honors us with her patronage, we now cater to the most distinguished clientele in the city.

ISABEL: They might even make your uncle a member of the Brotherhood of the Holy Blood.

JUAN: Christ almighty, Isabel, that's just not possible.

ISABEL: Well, you deserve it more than they do, even if you're not of noble birth.

JUAN: That's enough foolish talk.

ISABEL: And Anna, you'll be the first to benefit from the prosperity God has bestowed upon us by making a splendid marriage. You'll receive plenty of proposals. You're vivacious, intelligent, beautiful . . . actually, quite like your mother and me.

ANNA: *(To Juan)* Do you think I'm beautiful, too?

ISABEL: That's a question better left for the young men.

VINCENT: Stunning. . . .

BATISTA: Gorgeous. . . .

ISABEL: A young lady's greatest charms are her chastity and virtue, so if I ever catch wind of the slightest inconstancy, I'll beat the daylights out of you!

ANNA: Oh sure, when you were a young woman it was all right to display your charms in the river. . . . Oh, let me go washing with you! I want to hang some sheets and show off my bosom, too!

(She laughs.)

ISABEL: You're a shameless little flirt! Shameless!

(*Everyone laughs.*)

ANNA: So, when do we start rehearsing, uncle?

ISABEL: Never!

JUAN: Christ almighty, Isabel, how can you say that? Her Majesty the Vicereine is expecting a tremendous performance from us. She's always enjoyed the farces we've put on. Remember how she roared at Lope de Rueda's plays and at those other witty writers!

ISABEL: That old bag only laughs at the naughty bits.

JUAN: Well, life at court is very harsh. She deserves a little relief from the stress.

ISABEL: Some stress! Arranging balls, organizing hunts, building palaces . . . not to mention other, more insidious pastimes.

VINCENT: Don't forget her favorite sport: humiliating the poor.

JUAN: That's not true.

VINCENT: Oh no? What about the horrible way she crushed that rebellion of the artisan guilds.

JUAN: That was a long time ago. It's all forgotten now.

VINCENT: Forgotten by those who were killed, I can assure you.

ISABEL: A woman who has had three husbands!

BATISTA: One right after the other. . . .

ISABEL: Son, once a gal samples three different melons, it's hard for her not to want to taste the whole patch.

BATISTA: Mother, it's a sin to speak about the royals that way.

JUAN: Or their subjects. . . . Look, God has imparted an order to the world: the king above commoners, the priest above parishioners, and man above woman. Any attempt to alter divine will is a serious and unpardonable offense. The Vicereine is Our Royal Highness, and no one but God may condemn her behavior.

ISABEL: Oh sure, the nobles are truly noble, the bishops are all saints, and the viceroys are perfect.

VINCENT: While the rest of us are just lambs waiting to be fleeced for their profit, in return for a fistful of feed.

JUAN: Vincent, you take back those words this instant.

VINCENT: There's no way around it! I'm a lamb, too—I print what I'm told and wait for my ration of alfalfa.

BATISTA: I'm happy tanning hides to bind their books.

VINCENT: Those leaflets we print to keep the townspeople ignorant are starting to burn my hands. I often hate you, father, for the way you aid and abet all this.

JUAN: Vincent Timoneda, if I hadn't felt you kicking in your mother's womb and been present at your birth, I would not believe you were my son. Your mother and I have made a lot of sacrifices so you and your brother would have anything you needed. Through years of hard work, I managed to adapt my talents as a tanner to the difficult art of printing. The fact that the Vicereine or bishop or society should value my efforts and, as you so contemptuously put it, toss me a bigger ration of feed is a result of my producing wool in greater quantity and of better quality than any of my competitors. I, for one, am proud of my achievements.

VINCENT: And of how you've lined your pockets.

ISABEL: Those pockets are always open to you, don't ever forget that. You apologize to your father this instant for those unseemly words.

JUAN: There's no need for apologies. In this house my children are free to express their opinions.

BATISTA: I agree and always will agree with you, father.

JUAN: That's not what I want from you, Batista. I want you to be in agreement with yourself.

VINCENT: Father, are you?

ISABEL: Do you have the nerve to stand in judgment of your own father?

JUAN: *(To Vincent)* Honestly, I don't know. Don't think that question doesn't haunt me at times.

ANNA: Have you assigned the roles in the play yet?

JUAN: We'll get to that in a moment, Anna. Just let me finish what I have to say to Vincent. I read and write whatever I want, pieces for the theater, rigmaroles, poetry. I mount productions by various authors, and until now no one has put any restraints on my imagination or my work.

VINCENT: But don't you think that some day they'll ask you to repay their generosity by using your talent to serve their interests?

JUAN: Until now, theirs have coincided with mine.

VINCENT: And when they don't?

JUAN: When that day comes we'll pose the question again.

ANNA: I want to play the serving wench.

ISABEL: What? The tart who's sleeping with two married men and ends up rolling in the hay with a puppeteer?

ANNA: Why not?

ISABEL: My sister did not entrust her daughter to me so she'd end up some actress who accepts any old part, no matter how indecent.

ANNA: Anything to do with love is fine with me.

ISABEL: You call that "love"? Child, don't you see that the plot your dirty old uncle has cooked up is a scandalous attack on the dignity of all decent women?

ANNA: How so? If she's happy and makes the other three happy . . . ?

ISABEL: Hush up, for God's sake. You don't know what you're saying.

ANNA: Two young, dashing kings find out their wives are cheating on them. Aren't they right to seek comfort in an exciting young thing like a servant girl?

JUAN: *(Stepping onto the stage)* Quick upon leaving my castle at dawn, I made my horse turn tail for to fetch my lady's shawl, which I had left behind and was wont to carry with me into battle as a token tied to my crossbow. I mount the flight of stairs, enter the crenellated tower leading to the royal bedchamber, when what should I espy through the battlement window?

(To Batista, who joins in the scene.)

What is it you espy in your venerable bed, sire?

BATISTA: Is that not my faithful wife and lady?

JUAN: At least the buttocks look like hers.

BATISTA: And is that not the cursed kitchen humpback mounting her?

JUAN: Forsooth, his virile member is straighter than his shoulders.

BATISTA: Oh, I am wretched and forlorn! What unnatural holes must I cut into this royal crown to make room for my cuckold's horns?

JUAN: What ever will you do? Surrender not to impulse!

BATISTA: I shall kill her, kill her, kill her!

JUAN: To what avail, sire? The new queen would only betray you with another servant as soon as you turned your back.

BATISTA: Then I shan't kill her. You are right. I will turn tail again and this time make do without the shawl.

JUAN: Go off to war with your cousin, the king, and seek on the battlefield what peace you've failed to find in your rear guard.

VINCENT: *(Who has joined in the scene)* What ill has befallen you, cousin? You look haggard, sorrowful, despondent.

BATISTA: Oh, if you knew the depths of my misfortune!

JUAN: *(To Vincent)* Ask not, madman! Curiosity is ever the cause of man's suffering.

VINCENT: I have come for to fetch my wife's ruby necklace, which I wear twined about my arm to embolden me before mine enemies. Last night I placed it beneath her pillow. Pray, what is this? Curses and damnation! The royal bedroom door is locked!

BATISTA: And what espy you through the keyhole?

VINCENT: The rosy nipples of my beloved lady, and . . . no, this cannot be! Do you espy what I espy? Look you.

BATISTA: A man doth lick them like caramel candies.

VINCENT: No!

BATISTA: And descendeth ever lower down her flesh.

VINCENT: Go on.

BATISTA: Lower, lower . . .

VINCENT: How far?

BATISTA: He's gotten off now!

VINCENT: *(Covering the keyhole)* Oh, enough! *(Now he looks)* 'Tis the court jester! That ridiculous fellow who make us laugh in his outlandish motley.

BATISTA: One could not quite say he dresses so now, since the miscreant is buck naked.

VINCENT: Oh, no! I shall have revenge! I shall plunge my dagger into their hearts and dispatch my soul with the selfsame weapon.

JUAN: Good fortune has it that the door be locked, so your cousin may prevail upon you to reconsider.

VINCENT: Pray, what advice can he give me?

BATISTA: Go wage war without the rubies . . . and have them make more room in that crown.

JUAN: Don't lose heart, lads. Women are faithless and fickle by nature.

ISABEL: And men are little angels. Listen to him.

JUAN: That's different.

ISABEL: Well, just so you know, it serves those two striplings right that their wives are unfaithful.

JUAN: What are you talking about, you senseless woman?

ISABEL: Look at them. It's clear they're more worried about waging their little war and wearing the right accessories than they are about satisfying women.

ANNA: If my husband ever left me hungering, I swear to God I'd bolt down the first tasty dish that came my way.

ISABEL: Do you hear that, Juan?

ANNA: You were quick to make excuses for the wives, too, auntie.

ISABEL: Because they're queens, and queens are another story. You're my sister's girl, and when you marry you'll put up with what you have to, understand? Like all women do. Oh, if you only knew how starved I've been these last few years. . . .

JUAN: Do you mean to say you have some complaint with me?

ISABEL: You have to admit you're not very keen on action.

JUAN: Decent women like you and our niece have no need for such base pleasures.

ISABEL: Says you!

JUAN: Says me and a pile of books this thick by theologians, learned men, and church fathers.

ISABEL: Well, I have a little book, too, down here, that says just the opposite.

ANNA: You tell him, auntie. I have one, too.

ISABEL: You hush. You're an innocent child, and you haven't read page one yet.

ANNA: I have, too!

JUAN: On with the show!

VINCENT: My beloved, noble cousin, I have an idea!

BATISTA: I am all ears.

VINCENT: As we have been unable, despite zealous vigilance, to control our wives, who comfort themselves with other men the moment we leave them unguarded, let us share between us some pretty, openhanded lass. Thus shall she remain ever under the watchful eye of one of us.

BATISTA: And come night?

VINCENT: Come night she shall lie between us in bed so that no one may approach her from either side. Then, share and share alike . . . today for me, tomorrow for you!

BATISTA: But where ever shall we find so pleasing a beauty?

VINCENT: Why here, at this very inn. I've already set my sights on one.

BATISTA: You have a gift, cousin.

(They kiss exaggeratedly, like two women friends.)

BOTH: Mmmwwwaaahhh! Mmmwwwaaahhh!

JUAN: The innkeep, sires, at your service.

BATISTA: *(To Vincent)* This fat guy is your brilliant idea for gladdening our bed?

VINCENT: *(To Batista)* Wait. *(To Juan)* And your daughter?

(Anna joins in the scene.)

JUAN: Lass, welcome Their Lordships.

BATISTA: *(Stroking her chin)* Stunning . . .

VINCENT: And well endowed . . .

ANNA: Many thanks, Your Lordships. I will endeavor to repay your kindness with all my modest abilities.

(She sticks out her buttocks, and each caresses one cheek.)

ISABEL: Oh, no! Nobody is touching my niece's ass, least of all in public.

ANNA: But auntie, it's my cousins.

ISABEL: I don't care if it's the pope. *(She crosses herself)* All right, the pope maybe, but no one else.

JUAN: Isabel, please . . .

ISABEL: Do you expect this innocent creature to share a bed with two men? Isn't it true, angel, that you would never consent to such a thing?

ANNA: Well . . .

ISABEL: See? Look how reluctant the poor girl is! She's red with shame.

ANNA: I think I would. Yes, I think I would consent.

ISABEL: You don't know what you're saying.

ANNA: My cousins are pretty handsome.

ISABEL: And you're a misguided girl who doesn't know what wickedness is. That's enough theater for today! Anna, the dishes need washing in the kitchen. And take care not to touch that bottle of wine—it's already emptier than it should be. . . . The rest of you, go about your business. Let's see if we can't do a little work in this house for a change. Juan, you and your imagination will bring us all to ruin.

(Vincent walks toward the press, which he will later work. Batista prepares to tan hides.)

JUAN: But somebody has to play the serving wench! There are only a few days left before the festival.

ISABEL: You can forget about your niece. She is purity itself, and she'll take her purity to the altar, like all the young maids in our family. Like I did, remember?

JUAN: Barely. It was so many years ago.

ISABEL: You ingrate! When a woman surrenders a thing like that, she never forgets.

ANNA: *(Sighing)* It's true, uncle. She never forgets.

ISABEL: What would you know about it? Tread carefully, child. No wine and no romance, understand?

(She picks up a basket of clothes and exits. Juan heads toward the vine arbor and starts to write. Instead of walking toward the kitchen, Anna approaches Batista.)

ANNA: Whew! Auntie really gave me a scare there. What if she finds out you're the one who robbed me of my maidenhood?

BATISTA: Are you sure about that?

ANNA: How could you doubt me? You, the first and only man in my life . . . you, to whom I gave myself spotless and without stain like a lily in an Easter parade.

BATISTA: What do you expect me to say? The first time we took that tumble in the grass, your portals of pleasure opened so wide I slipped right in without the slightest effort. And that, people say, is not natural.

ANNA: When a woman's love is as great as the love I feel for you, what's natural is to make the going easy.

BATISTA: I don't trust my brother, of whom you're so fond. He's always hanging around, and he follows you everywhere. . . . I even caught him hugging you out by the hayfield.

ANNA: I already explained that to you. He saw us lying together by the farm-house once and threatened to tell auntie everything. I have no choice but to be a little friendly toward him.

BATISTA: What do you mean, "friendly"?

ANNA: Oh, nothing, stupid little things. A quick peck, a soft caress, a wink . . .

BATISTA: That's all?

ANNA: He tried to feel my titty once, but I slapped him.

BATISTA: Nice going!

ANNA: This one . . . no, this one! See? I don't even remember. All right? You're the only man I love.

BATISTA: Let's get married then.

ANNA: What, a wedding between cousins? That would be incest, and we'd both be damned to hell for all eternity. Besides, your parents want me to marry a gentleman. I can't go against their wishes after all they've done for me.

BATISTA: But what will become of us then?

ANNA: I'll come visit the family from time to time . . . and stretch out on the garden grass . . .

VINCENT: *(From his workspace)* Anna! Bring me some water.

ANNA: Coming!

BATISTA: My brother again! He doesn't leave you alone for a second.

ANNA: Have a little patience. If you only knew what I go through to put up with him.

BATISTA: Then it's true you don't like him?

ANNA: That guy? Not a bit. But I do have to pretend.

BATISTA: Ten o'clock in the garden?

ANNA: I wouldn't miss it.

VINCENT: Where's that water?

ANNA: It's coming! Uh, what a man!

(Batista returns to his work while Anna approaches Vincent.)

VINCENT: What do you have to talk to him about?

ANNA: I need to keep the act up, Vincent my love. If you only knew what I go through to put up with him.

VINCENT: Why did you let him nibble on your neck then?

ANNA: I can't go against his wishes. You don't want him to tell auntie how he caught us rolling in the hay.

VINCENT: I'd almost prefer it.

ANNA: Silly, you're the only man I love. . . . What's an innocent pat on the hand or neck anyhow?

VINCENT: Are you sure he'll be content with that?

ANNA: He tried to feel my titty once, but I slapped him.

VINCENT: That dirty dog!

ANNA: This one . . . no, this one! See, I don't even remember. He's only a kid.

VINCENT: An ass-kissing dimwit, that's what he is. Always agreeing with my parents or the Vicereine and lifting his heart up to the Lord. He annoys me.

ANNA: How different the two of you are! You're a real man. I'm proud I lost my virginity to you.

VINCENT: We'll talk about that in a minute . . .

ANNA: Not again? Are you trying to make me angry?

VINCENT: It was just too easy. Everyone knows a woman's maidenhead is a tough nut to crack.

ANNA: Not for an impetuous guy like you who bowls over whatever stands in his way!

VINCENT: Then why don't we leave this house, find a priest who'll marry us, and buy a plot of land where we can raise our children?

ANNA: I'd like nothing more! I swear to you, my love, even after I marry a rich landowner like auntie and uncle wish, you'll always be my favorite. Should I bring you that water?

VINCENT: Only that body and those lips can quench this thirst. Ten o'clock, then?

ANNA: Better make that eleven. I have to finish my housework.

VINCENT: Is Batista part of your "housework"?

ANNA: What a dirty mind you have.

VINCENT: The barn, as usual?

ANNA: I'll be there.
> *(Vincent caresses her buttocks.)*
Don't touch me like that. Once I get all hot and bothered I can't sit still.
> *(Vincent starts to work. Anna walks toward Juan, who is writing beneath the vine arbor, and flirtatiously covers his eyes with her hands.)*

ANNA: Guess who!

JUAN: Leave me be!

ANNA: Why are you always so mean to your loving niece?

JUAN: You know perfectly well.

ANNA: Perhaps I didn't satisfy you?

JUAN: For the love of God, Annie, don't play games with me. That only happened . . . because the devil won the day, but it will never happen again.

ANNA: I don't think bringing me to glory was the devil's doing.

JUAN: Well, if not his, then whose? It was a very warm night, and with the scent of those damned orange blossoms wafting through the house . . .

ANNA: Mmmm! I think I can still smell them . . .

JUAN: I heard a voice coming from your bedroom—it was you, talking in your sleep. You woke with a start, and your heart was beating under your nightgown like an innocent runaway colt. . . .

ANNA: You were making my heart thump, not the nightmare.

JUAN: I tried to calm you, like I would have some frightened little girl. . . .

ANNA: Well, you failed. Your hot breath, moist skin, and warm hands made me more and more excited.

JUAN: I let the thrill of the moment carry me away like a schoolboy.

ANNA: It wasn't the thrill that pulled you softly on top of me. It was my hands.

JUAN: Let's forget this happy event once and for all, shall we?

ANNA: Whatever you say, sir, but that won't be easy. It was so wonderful!

JUAN: Don't you understand? Your mother entrusted you to us to keep out of harm's way. . . . And it was I, of all people, who took your virginity from you!

ANNA: No one could have done it more gently or sweetly.

JUAN: That's enough. Don't say anything more.

ANNA: So, was it good for you? Did I satisfy your manly desires with my clumsy girlish ways?

JUAN: No!

ANNA: Then why did you come back a few days later? The devil again?

JUAN: No doubt, but now I'm on my guard against his tricks.

ANNA: They say three times is a charm. . . . I'll leave my door open every night just in case.

JUAN: You needn't bother.

ANNA: And pray to all the saints that I'll hear your muffled steps outside my room again very soon.

JUAN: I ought to take you back home so you'll be safe from these temptations.

ANNA: And who would look after me there? My mother is dead.

JUAN: I don't want to be responsible for you anymore. What would your aunt say if she found out what's happened?

ANNA: Stop worrying. She sleeps like a log until sunup. I can hear her snoring from my room. . . . You, on the other hand, I hear tossing and turning all night. . . . Is it I, perchance, who robs you of your sleep?

JUAN: Leave me in peace!

(Transition)

ANNA: What are you writing?

JUAN: The usual. Stories and novellas I call "rigmaroles."

ANNA: How do you think up all these things?

JUAN: Occasionally, a person who's not from these parts will tell me some, others I come up with myself.

ANNA: For the life of me, uncle, I can't figure you out. Who are you, really? The man who makes up these stories, or that mean old hothead who wants to kick me out of his house so I won't disturb his peace or besmirch the family honor?

JUAN: I'm two people at once, like all men.

ANNA: I still don't understand. Why don't you explain it to me again.

JUAN: Look, it's very simple. Make-believe is one thing and reality another. Just like the madness of our dreams is one thing while everyday truth is something else entirely. Is it clear now?

ANNA: I'm more confused than ever.

JUAN: You'll see, Annie. . . . I was born in a hovel, as you know, and I went hungry and suffered from the cold many times as a boy. I took more hard knocks than I have hairs on my head. But now, as you can see, I have my own print shop and my own stone house and am an upstanding citizen in the community who one day will marry off his niece to a rich landowner.

ANNA: And . . . ?

JUAN: Well, that's the truth of our lives, the only truth you and I have . . . everything else *(pointing to his writing)* is just paper that will burn up faster than you can say "Hail Mary."

ANNA: And what were those two nights to you, make-believe or reality?

JUAN: I would say they were my wildest dreams.

ANNA: Will they also have to burn up in a "Hail Mary"?

JUAN: I'm afraid so.

ANNA: For a writer, you're a lousy liar, uncle.

JUAN: How dare you!

ANNA: Truth, for you, is the exact opposite of what you say it is.

JUAN: You think so?

ANNA: For you, reality is those rigmaroles and the creaky floorboards outside my room. And Auntie Isabel's snoring, your family honor, and the Vicereine's financial backing are what's make-believe. You ought to light a torch and reduce all that to ashes.

JUAN: Have you lost your senses? If we always gave in to our urges, we'd be no better than the animals.

ANNA: But if you repress those urges, you'll be no better than a piece of charred coal.

JUAN: Let me do my writing.

ANNA: For goodness sake, uncle, have some courage! Don't give up on living!

JUAN: You crazy girl!

ANNA: Or on loving me.

(She embraces him as Isabel enters.)

ISABEL: Good news from the laundry! *(Seeing her niece)* What are you doing?

ANNA: I . . . was just leaving. *(She exits toward the kitchen, passing close to Vincent, who embraces her.)*

JUAN: Won't the lot of you let me work for one moment?

ISABEL: Stop grousing and listen to this.

JUAN: More fishwife gossip?

ISABEL: What if I were to tell you that one of the maids from the Court Secretary's palace who was washing right beside me in the river let me in on a little secret?

JUAN: I would reply, why don't you tell me later?

ISABEL: Fine. Your loss. *(She begins folding the clothes in her basket.)*

ANNA: *(To Vincent)* Enough already, Vincent, I can't breathe. You're squeezing me to death.

VINCENT: What were you saying to the old man?

ANNA: What's it to you? Besides, he's not that old.

VINCENT: I can overlook that kind of stuff with my brother, which is already a lot to ask, but if I ever catch you making a move on him, I'll kill you.

ANNA: Don't tell me you're jealous of your own father?

VINCENT: I'm jealous of my own shadow.

ANNA: Jesus! How can I convince you *(pointing to her heart)* that there's no one but you in here? *(They embrace, when the press suddenly begins making strange noises because Vincent has been distracted from his work. Anna runs off horrified.)*

VINCENT: Father! Father! Come quickly!

JUAN: *(Approaching)* What have you done? How are you ever going to be a master printer if you don't pay attention to your work? Look, the platen is broken. This will set back deliveries by at least a week.

ISABEL: Your father is right, Vincent. You should be more careful.

VINCENT: I don't like this line of work. I don't like what we're printing.

JUAN: And for that you wreck the machinery?

VINCENT: Some day I'll only publish what I want.

JUAN: Once you have your own shop, you can do as you please, but I'm in charge here, and if you don't like it you can march straight out that door. Understand me?

ISABEL: For God's sake, Juan.

JUAN: You be quiet. *(To Batista, who is tanning hides very noisily)* And you, enough with that ear-splitting racket!

BATISTA: Whatever you say, father. *(He heads toward the kitchen while Juan walks toward the broken machine.)*

VINCENT: Where are you going?

BATISTA: To the kitchen.

VINCENT: To look for Anna? Chasing her skirt all day?

BATISTA: That makes two of us. I want her to bring me a glass of water.

ISABEL: Is everyone in this house thirsty today?

BATISTA: It must be the heat. *(He exits) (The sound of a bell freezes the action.)*

JUAN: What's that bell?

ISABEL: The front gate.

JUAN: But it's always open.

ISABEL: Then it must be a courtesy call.

JUAN: At this hour?

ISABEL: If you ever paid any attention to me, maybe you'd learn a few things you can't find in your precious books. *(They ring again.)*

JUAN: They're ringing again.

ISABEL: *(Shouting)* Anna, go welcome the Secretary to the Vicereine.

JUAN: You know who it is?

ISABEL: I may be a stupid woman, but even though I can't read or write, I'm still smarter than all of you. Anna!

(Anna enters out of breath, lowering her skirt, followed by Batista.)

ANNA: Coming, auntie!

VINCENT: Hey, what were you doing?

BATISTA: Drying my hands.

VINCENT: On her skirt? I'm going to give you such a . . .

BATISTA: Go on, I dare you!

ISABEL: It's touching to watch the two brothers defend their cousin's honor. See, Juan? People here in Valencia are more decent than the characters in your scandalous farces.

JUAN: Right you are, Isabel. You're the smartest one in the house.

(Downstage beneath the vine arbor, Anna has shown in the Secretary to the Court.)

ANNA: This way, Excellency. Sit here under the arbor where it's cool.

SECRETARY: Thank you, child. . . . Your name is Anna, correct?

ANNA: At your service, Excellency. How did you know?

SECRETARY: I know more about you than you might imagine.

ANNA: Your Excellency is too kind. I'll let my uncle know you're here.

ISABEL: *(To Batista)* Go fetch your father's nice coat. The news he's bringing may be important.

JUAN: And how would you know what he's come to tell me?

ISABEL: The palace maid heard the Secretary talking. It's about Anna.

JUAN: Our niece?

ISABEL: And about the Brotherhood of the Holy Blood you so want to be a part of.

JUAN: What has one got to do with the other?

ISABEL: That girl may be the key that unlocks doors for you.

JUAN: But . . . ?

ISABEL: He's a widower, and from the looks of it the man is completely smitten with the young thing. Go on, don't keep him waiting. In the meantime, we'll pray to St. Fulgentius for succor.

(Juan has put on his coat and walks downstage.)

ISABEL: *(Crossing herself)* Oh, blessed St. Fulgentius, may

Your charity this day impart

Consolement to a sinner's heart,

For this great mercy I thee pray.

VINCENT: I have to fix that platen.

BATISTA: And I have to tan those hides.

ISABEL: Oh, no! We'll have none of that. On your knees and pray!

(They all pray.)

SECRETARY: My good Juan Timoneda.

JUAN: Excellency, welcome. *(To Anna)* Bring out a jug of our best wine to refresh the Lord Secretary.

SECRETARY: Much obliged. *(Anna exits)* Beautiful girl, a real sight for sore eyes. . . .

JUAN: A treasure, Excellency.

SECRETARY: The very embodiment of our beloved land. She seems to stow in her eyes the light of our sun and the golden glow of our orange groves.

JUAN: I see that the years have not diminished your taste for pretty girls.

SECRETARY: Don't exaggerate now, my dear Juan, I just turned fifty . . . some time ago, to be sure, but my heart . . .

JUAN: *(Laughing)* Ah, your heart . . .

SECRETARY: As young and frisky as a lad's. My legs, however . . . do you see? My legs are quite another story. They seem to have borne the weight of all my years.

JUAN: It's the humidity of our climate, Excellency, and not your years.

SECRETARY: Right. The humidity. You are a very clever man, Juan Timoneda.

JUAN: Oh, please, Excellency . . .

SECRETARY: And these fine qualities must be recognized. . . . Ah, here comes the wine with its lovely server. *(Anna has entered and serves them.)* Won't you take a drink with us, sweet dove?

JUAN: Her lips have never touched wine. She is an innocent babe.

ANNA: Of course, for you I could make an exception.

SECRETARY: Do, by all means. Let's see how it sits with you.

ANNA: Thank you, Excellency. *(She lifts the glass and empties it in a swig, to the Secretary's amazement.)*

SECRETARY: Oh, my. . . . How was it?

ANNA: Delicious.

SECRETARY: Look, look at the little bird. . . .

JUAN: Don't make her blush, Excellency.

ANNA: May I go now?

SECRETARY: Against all my wishes, but I am afraid what your uncle and I have to speak about is not for your charming ears. Not for the moment, at least.

ANNA: At your service, Excellency. *(She exits with a respectful curtsy.)*

SECRETARY: A virgin?

JUAN: And then some! Her simplicity is truly touching.

SECRETARY: No doubt she has her admirers?

JUAN: Younger men don't interest her, I can assure you.

SECRETARY: Ah, no?

JUAN: Every once in a while, very rarely, when some young fellow shows up with business at the shop, she looks as though she has seen the devil.

SECRETARY: Well, I commend her good sense. These young bucks today are not to be trusted.

JUAN: I don't think she cares how spry a man's legs are. What matters to her is how spry his heart is.

SECRETARY: A very sensible girl.

JUAN: Besides . . . Oh, I don't know whether I should tell you. . . .

SECRETARY: Do tell. . . .

JUAN: Well, the other night she confided to her aunt that you were the most handsome and dashing man she had ever seen in her life.

SECRETARY: *(Puffing up like a peacock)* Oh, at one time, I wouldn't say I wasn't . . .

JUAN: For Christ's sake, man, you're fitter than ever! There's not a wrinkle on your face.

SECRETARY: *(With false modesty)* Oh, perhaps one or two. . . . But getting back to Annie, she truly is a girl of many charms. . . .

JUAN: And in all the right sizes and places!

SECRETARY: Indeed. Hee, hee, hee. *(Laughing like a rabbit)* You've noticed them, too?

JUAN: As her uncle . . . only as her uncle. You should see her wearing the dress she had made for the festival!

SECRETARY: What's it like?

JUAN: Well, from the front it drapes down like this . . . *(Tracing the neckline)*

SECRETARY: Down to here? *(Tracing quite a low neckline)*

JUAN: More . . . or less. While from behind . . . *(Pointing to his rear)*

SECRETARY: Oh, tell me what it's like from behind!

JUAN: *(Cutting him off)* By the way, speaking of the festival, have you brought the order for the pages we're to publish?

SECRETARY: Of course. And paid in advance, as always.

JUAN: This year I thought we might put out four or five leaflets with stories of romance, battle, and adventure that will leave our readers feeling happy as princes.

SECRETARY: That will be a great cost to our treasury.

JUAN: Forgive me if I seem forward, but to my mind we can never do enough to honor our most honorable brotherhood, which I so admire and revere.

SECRETARY: And of which you ought to be a member.

JUAN: I'm not worthy of such an honor.

SECRETARY: You may count on my help and on the support of Our Lady the Vicereine who, as you know, is the Head . . . Brother.

JUAN: But my family is lowborn. . . .

SECRETARY: True, but let's say that your niece—and I just use her as an example—should make a match with a man of noble birth. . . . Do you follow?

JUAN: Right behind you, Excellency.

SECRETARY: Five leaflets, you say? That is quite a lot of money, but so be it.

JUAN: Oh, thank you! *(Calling out)* More wine for His Excellency!

SECRETARY: Now with respect to the brotherhood. . . . The chapter will reconvene in a few days, and I assure you I will keep your wishes very much in mind. *(Isabel enters with a jug of wine.)*

ISABEL: Lord Secretary . . .

JUAN: What are you doing here?

ISABEL: The wine.

JUAN: Where's the girl?

ISABEL: In the kitchen. Where else would she be? Shall I serve you, my lord?

SECRETARY: No, thank you. My thirst has suddenly vanished.

ISABEL: I only wanted to curtsy before His Excellency and welcome him to our humble home. Everything here is at His Excellency's disposal. Everything!

SECRETARY: I am most happy to hear that. I have changed my mind. You may pour me a bit more of that refreshing wine.

ISABEL: *(Pouring)* With extreme pleasure.

SECRETARY: I am going to tell you both something in confidence. Ever since my wife passed away, I have been very lonely in the palace. You cannot imagine how cold the nights can be in such a large bedroom in so spacious a bed. Oh, Juan, how I envy your slumber beside a wife as warm and plump as yours.

JUAN: I lend her to you gladly, Excellency.

SECRETARY: For heaven's sake, don't joke like that. I have no one but middle-aged men to attend me, and they are all skinny, depressing, and almost always suffering from colds.

ISABEL: That's very touching. . . .

SECRETARY: Which is why I believe that the company of a cheerful and virtuous young maid would brighten up the entire palace like some little songbird.

ISABEL: You wouldn't be cold in bed. *(They laugh.)*

JUAN: So, have you found the lucky woman who possesses such charms?

SECRETARY: Yes. Your niece.

ISABEL: Our Anna? *(Very fake)* My, what a surprise!

SECRETARY: I hope this does not displease you. . . .

JUAN: On the contrary, Excellency. We are truly honored.

ISABEL: But he'll be depriving us of the angel's sweet company. . . . *(Crying)* Oh, how empty this house will be without her!

SECRETARY: I hope the Brothers of the Holy Blood will manage to console your husband . . . and you, perhaps, might better bear your sorrow in the new washbasin with the water main I'll have built right here in your front yard.

ISABEL: But what about my two boys? They're going to miss their cousin something awful. The three were raised like brothers and sister.

SECRETARY: We will arrange for some little thing to console them as well. Now why don't we drink to your charming niece's health?

(They drink.)

ISABEL: So, have you set a date for the wedding?

SECRETARY: *(Choking on the wine)* What wedding?

ISABEL: But . . .

SECRETARY: My good woman, I can't simply remarry only months after becoming a widower. My lofty position obliges me to adhere to certain social norms, which I am neither willing nor able to contravene, and a long, strict period of mourning for the passing of a model Christian wife is one of these. Your niece will have to observe it, too.

JUAN: Of course.

ISABEL: Is it your intention, God forgive me, to cohabit with a virtuous maid from a decidedly virtuous family?

JUAN: Now woman . . .

ISABEL: Do you take my niece for a slut?

JUAN: For Christ's sake, Isabel, that word . . .

ISABEL: You social climber! You'd sell your soul to the devil to become a member of that beloved brotherhood.

JUAN: What are you trying to do, make a fool of me in front of the Secretary and the entire court?

ISABEL: It's my niece he wants to mount, not yours!

JUAN: Quiet!

ISABEL: Look here, Lord Secretary, I've been washing clothes in the river all my life, and I'm used to it by now. So as far as I'm concerned, you can take your washbasin and water main and stick them where you please!

JUAN: You're coming off a bit uncouth. Pay her no attention, Excellency.

SECRETARY: My dear woman, no girl who wasn't proper and respectable could ever enter service in my house. If I took your niece to be a woman of the streets, as you insinuate, I would never have made you this proposition.

JUAN: See? Now hush up and don't comment on matters you don't understand.

SECRETARY: I can assure you, madam, that good luck has come calling at your door today.

ISABEL: Well, let it go back to its own door! An innocent child like my Anna!

JUAN: And if we don't heed the call . . . ?

SECRETARY: Fortune and disgrace are two sides of the same coin. So what shall it be, heads or tails?

ISABEL: I'll speak to the Vicereine. She's a woman, and she'll understand our refusal.

SECRETARY: I would never have taken such a step without her approval. Our Lady has been fully apprised of this matter and gives it her unqualified blessing.

ISABEL: And the Patriarch?

SECRETARY: He can say what he pleases. Everyone knows the Patriarch is a fanatic who finds sin everywhere he looks.

ISABEL: Of course, now that I think about it, if you do marry her once the period of mourning ends . . .

SECRETARY: My wedding, should I ever choose to marry again, would also have to be approved by the Vicereine, and, of course, she would never give her blessing if the bride's family did not enjoy the rank of nobility.

JUAN: Which we, as you well know, do not.

SECRETARY: Have no fear. Your niece will be allowed to continue in our service, respected by all, including my future wife, whoever she may be.

ISABEL: Let us at least speak with the girl. . . .

SECRETARY: I eagerly await your decision. Tomorrow, then.

JUAN: Please thank the Vicereine for her kind favors.

ISABEL: What favors? This is all we need!

SECRETARY: *(Kissing Isabel's hand, as if she were a noblewoman)* Delicious wine, my lady . . .

ISABEL: Lord Secretary . . .

SECRETARY: Oh, and just one more thing. It will not be fitting for your sweet niece to perform in the play. What would people say if they saw a girl in my personal service prancing about making obscene gestures onstage?

JUAN: But we've never done that.

SECRETARY: Then please do, so the Vicereine and I and everyone at court can enjoy a few hearty laughs. Hee, hee, hee . . . *(He exits)*

ISABEL: What does that son of a . . . strumpet take us for, anyhow?

JUAN: For what we are, Isabel, court jesters, no more and no less. We're of service because we amuse them when they're bored, spread their ideas with our presses, and warm their beds when the august ladies of their own class can't satisfy them. The more they humiliate us, the more we're in their debt because it's a privilege for commoners like you and me to let them enjoy our daughters, impose their will on us, and laugh at our farces.

ISABEL: That's horrible, Juan.

JUAN: The big fish in the Mediterranean eat the little ones, too. It's just that, for some reason, people are supposed to consider it an honor as long as the fish have gold scales and wear crowns on their heads. And even after they devour us, we're expected to thank them for the favor and wish them *bon appétit*.

ISABEL: What are you going to do?

JUAN: What can I do, Isabel?

ISABEL: What the laundresses do when someone insults us . . . crack him over the head with a washing pole!

JUAN: Talk is cheap. Even you got used to that old codger touching your bottom from time to time.

ISABEL: Maybe I liked it. . . . No, you're right. I didn't dare cross him for fear I'd lose my job.

JUAN: See?

ISABEL: Hold me, Juan.

JUAN: Oh, woman!

ISABEL: I know my body doesn't make you feel what you used to, but please, I need this now. I feel so insignificant, so humbled . . .

JUAN: *(Taking hold of her)* Like this?

ISABEL: We're not pieces of trash, Juan, I don't care what that pig says. My body is flabby, and maybe my mind has gone soft, too, from all the soap and water I've handled in my life, but I'm still your wife, the wife of the most handsome and talented man in the city. When those impotent, fancy jack-a-dandies are long forgotten, your genius will be remembered for generations to come, even outside Valencia, and thousands of people will read the stories you write under our vine arbor. That's why I wanted you to hold me, so I could cling tight to your greatness . . . and feel it so near me and yet so far away.

JUAN: Are you turning into a poet on me?

ISABEL: Don't make fun. I only know how to wash clothes. I haven't done anything else since I was a girl, but I swear to you that no woman leaves a sheet whiter than I do.

JUAN: Are you crying?

ISABEL: From rage! We brought up our niece to marry a gentleman, not to make some decrepit old coot's pecker stiff! No! No, no, no!

JUAN: You're a rebel, all right. Now I see where Vincent gets his anger.

ISABEL: I would've fought beside the artisans in their uprising, you'd better believe it.

JUAN: And what good would that have done? They were defeated, humiliated, wiped out. . . . Behind all their silk finery, gentlefolk conceal shackles, pain, and blood.

ISABEL: Well, we'll have to stand up to them and bring them down.

JUAN: That's just not possible, woman. There isn't a place in the land where their long swords couldn't stick us in the ass.

ISABEL: All right, Sir Know-It-All, then tell me, what do we do now?

JUAN: Why, rejoice in the great honor of being chosen for degradation.

ISABEL: But Juan . . .

JUAN: What else can we do? Bow low to the ground, smile at them—but in a submissive way so no one will think we're trying to be their equals—place our press at their disposal, entertain them onstage with racy plays so they can laugh and think they're virtuous. . . . Follow behind them in orderly fashion so they can march at the head of processions, applaud whenever they fart, and congratulate them when their noble old phalluses penetrate the fresh, young body of a peasant girl offered up like some lovely Christmas goose . . . all the while improving our lot, hoarding the ducats they drop from carefree hands, receiving certificates of honor that bear their signatures and seals . . . in a word, debase ourselves like poor fools to garner a modicum of honor and win the right to an honorable life with our crafty ways.

ISABEL: Is it this way everywhere?

JUAN: Maybe there are heroes in some corner of the globe who'd prefer death before dishonor, but I'm not one of them. Neither are you. I don't think my sons are, either. Or Anna, for that matter. What are you laughing at?

ISABEL: (Freeing herself from his embrace) My only consolation is knowing that we're handing him the sluttiest virgin in the realm.

JUAN: Ah, then you know. . . .

ISABEL: I snore at night because my nose stops up, not my ears.

JUAN: See what I mean? This is one of the few small pleasures they allow us . . . spoiling their schemes with tricks of our own.
(Both laugh.)

ISABEL: By the way, now that you've touched my body again after so long a time, what did you think of it?

JUAN: You were right, as usual. It is a bit flabby.

ISABEL: I bet my niece's is pretty firm.

JUAN: Yours was, too, at her age.

(A bell starts ringing.)

ISABEL: Vespers already? The afternoon has really flown by.

JUAN: Call everyone for prayers.

ISABEL: Vincent! Batista! Anna! Stop your work! It's vespers!

(The three appear.)

JUAN: Let us pray for Our Lady the Vicereine.

ISABEL: On top of everything else, we have to pray for her?

JUAN: Let us pray, too, for all the souls at court and especially for the Lord Secretary, who has deigned to honor our house this day with his . . . predilection.

ISABEL: The dirty louse.

ANNA: Him? How come?

ISABEL: Quiet now, we'll talk later.

JUAN: May the Mother of God and all the saints bless them for evermore. Amen.

ALL: Amen.

ISABEL: That's your father!

JUAN: Hail Mary, full of grace . . .

ALL: Amen.

ISABEL: That's your father for you!

(The bells continue ringing as they pray.)

CURTAIN

Act II

The same setting. Curtains suspended from poles have been draped over the stage, giving it the look of a small theater. The rehearsal proceeds from the point at which Vincent and Batista previously left off, with funny-looking crowns, cuckold's horns, and Juan Timoneda wearing an innkeeper's apron and cap.

BATISTA: You have a gift, cousin.

(They kiss exaggeratedly, like two women friends.)

BOTH: Mmmwwwaaahhh! Mmmwwwaaahhh!

JUAN: The innkeep, sires, at your service.

BATISTA: *(To Vincent)* This fat guy is your brilliant idea for gladdening our bed?

VINCENT: *(To Batista)* Wait. *(To Juan)* And your daughter?

JUAN: Here she comes. Lass, welcome Their Lordships.

(Purity appears.)

BATISTA: *(Stroking her chin)* Stunning . . .

VINCENT: And well endowed . . .

PURITY: Many thanks, Your Lordships. I will endeavor to repay your kindness with all my modest abilities.

(They touch her buttocks, each on one cheek.)

JUAN: *(Taking off his cap)* Excellent! Now the dancing begins.

(He sings and directs their movements. Background music may be heard.)

Tra la la, tra la la . . . a little more spirited! Look lively now! More smiling, more laughing! I want to hear laughter! Like at a wedding feast, get it?

PURITY: *(Stopping)* No, sir, I don't.

JUAN: What do you mean, you don't? Weddings are festive occasions. People feel merry, they dance. . . . Won't you be happy on your wedding day?

PURITY: Oh, I'll be mad with joy when my Aniceto returns from the Indies and we can be married. He's a soldier, you know.

JUAN: And when the big day comes, won't you be dancing all delighted and gay?

PURITY: I'll be mad with joy, for sure, but not so crazed that I'd waste my time shimmying. The way that brute is, after so many years apart, as soon as he sees me it'll be bataboom!, straight to the sack! My Aniceto is not too big on dancing.

JUAN: I can understand that, but after the two of you have tested the mattress, a little dancing . . .

PURITY: That's a laugh! I can see you don't know my Aniceto. How could we dance with that kind of back pain? We'll be lucky to be standing!
(She laughs.)

JUAN: Look, let's forget about your Aniceto . . .

PURITY: Forget about my Aniceto? I'll hang myself first.

JUAN: Just for the moment, woman. You'll understand. It's like a wedding, see?

PURITY: But with two grooms.

JUAN: Something like that.

PURITY: You call that a wedding?

JUAN: That's enough. Just do as I say. . . . You're an actress, and you have to learn to take direction.

PURITY: Oh no, now you listen here—I don't go for any of that stuff. I only came because the Lord Secretary asked me to, and I can't refuse the Lord Secretary anything. But I will not allow you to take me for something I am not. Actresses are looked down upon and aren't even buried in hallowed ground. Besides, I have my own profession.

JUAN: Don't I know it!

PURITY: I'm a prostitute, which, when you say it just like that, doesn't sound like a big deal, but if I rattled off the names of all the important people in the parish and at court whom I have serviced in my bed, you would be amazed! Sometimes I'm sorry I didn't keep a book with all their autographs! That's why I'm honored that the Lord Secretary, whom your niece now serves as mistress of the house, has extended me his friendship. It's true, the man has really made me work for it—I mean, just between you and me, he's not the easiest guy to—but do you know why he always picks me when he comes to the brothel? It isn't nice to say, but a girl who is out to serve has a lot of self-respect, and when something is asked of her, one way or the other she ends up providing it.

JUAN: That's enough stories for now—let's dance. You're happy, affectionate, dreamy . . .

PURITY: And after we dance they're going to take me to bed, one guy on each side?

JUAN: That's the play.

PURITY: The two of them are going to screw me, one after the other?

JUAN: That's the plot.

PURITY: Well, you'd better start looking for another girl because I'm not going to stand for that. I'm still a virgin.

JUAN: A virgin, in your line of work?

PURITY: What's so strange about that? There are lots of ways to make men happy. . . . But this right here *(pointing to her crotch)*, I'm saving this baby from the slightest damage because if my Aniceto returns and doesn't find everything in place, the way that animal is, he'll kick my ass but good.

JUAN: That's enough chitchat. Let's get down to work. Cue the music. Everyone is dancing and laughing. *(Music and dancing)* I want to hear those laughs, that's it, that's it, louder, louder!

(Anna's entrance interrupts the dancing. She is decked out in fine clothes.)

ANNA: God be with Your Lordships!

JUAN: Annie!

BATISTA: Look how elegant you are!

VINCENT: And how lovely!

(They surround her, happy to see her again.)

ISABEL: *(Feeling the fabric of her clothing)* Italian brocade, exquisite. When it needs cleaning, I'll hand wash it for you myself.

JUAN: So, how are they treating you at the Secretary's palace?

ANNA: Like a queen! We have chicken and roast suckling pig every day, wine that's chilled in snow from the mountaintops, carriage rides, music at soirées, linen sheets . . .

ISABEL: And . . . what else?

ANNA: Nothing else.

ISABEL: Nothing nothing else?

ANNA: Little little else. Very little little else. I really miss this house!

BATISTA: Remember the smell of the orange trees in our garden?

ANNA: I can't get it out of my mind.

VINCENT: And the animals in the barn you always liked so much?

ANNA: I fall asleep every night thinking of them and the fragrance of hay in their stalls.

JUAN: This is Purity. She's come to perform the part you were going to play.

PURITY: Mistress, it is an honor . . .

ANNA: *(Holding out her hand to be kissed)* Child . . .

ISABEL: Bring our Anna a chair. *(Batista brings one)* Fruit from the garden?

VINCENT: A little wine?

ANNA: No, thank you, I'm stuffed. You're all very gracious.

JUAN: It's nothing you don't deserve. By the way, have you found out when the chapter of the brotherhood is meeting?

ANNA: No, but the Lord Secretary asked me to give you this *(handing him a sack of coins)* to pay for the new publications. And this satin ribbon is a present for you, auntie. *(She gives it to Isabel.)*

ISABEL: It's beautiful. God bless you.

JUAN: *(To Vincent)* Bring her the first batch of leaflets we've printed.

BATISTA: I'm giving you a jewel box of Florentine leather to keep your gems in. I've already made a dozen to sell to the ladies at court.

ISABEL: I'm so glad to see you this happy!

ANNA: I'm the happiest woman in the world, and I owe it all to you.

JUAN: Are you really, Annie? I fear I detect a tinge of melancholy in your eyes.

ANNA: Any day now they're going to present you with the medallion of the Holy Blood, auntie has her satin ribbon, you're printing more pages now than you ever did, the ladies at court will buy Batista's Florentine leather jewel boxes at inflated prices—what do any of you care what's happening in my eyes?

ISABEL: Oh, but we do.

ANNA: I would like to speak to the girl now. Please leave us alone.

ISABEL: Anna!

JUAN: We don't deserve to be treated this way. We always did everything for you.

ANNA: Leave us, I beg you. I command you!

JUAN: Come. Let's go.

(*Everyone except Purity moves to the back of the stage.*)

PURITY: Tough, huh?

ANNA: Impossible is more like it.

PURITY: Nothing is impossible for you, my lady. You're young and beautiful, and you have rosy skin and soft lips . . .

ANNA: What can I say?

PURITY: The palace is massive and gloomy and dark . . .

ANNA: And very cold.

PURITY: Why kid ourselves about the Lord Secretary? He's nothing but a frosty old bag of bones.

ANNA: It would have to be the one soft thing on his body! Tender as a newborn babe, and always asleep like one.

PURITY: And that bed is so large . . .

ANNA: From what I hear, you're quite familiar with it.

PURITY: Uh! I could draw you that damask pattern on the canopy from memory.

ANNA: I know he went to the brothel the other night.

PURITY: No, he didn't, I swear it! Ever since he has known Your Ladyship, it would never occur to him to look for meaningless consolation from some slut.

ANNA: One of the servants who accompanied him gave me the whole story.

PURITY: He was lying.

ANNA: I'm not blaming you. Your job requires you to take on all comers. . . . So, were you successful?

PURITY: Again, my lady . . .

ANNA: Did you manage to light his wick with even the smallest of flames?

PURITY: I don't understand you.

ANNA: Did you succeed in waking that tiny newborn babe?

PURITY: I still don't understand.

ANNA: Did he fuck you? Good Lord, people really have to spell things out for you!

PURITY: I can assure you I have an easier time satisfying a ship's crew than I do milking two or three drops out of that body.

ANNA: I'd also prefer to take on a ship's crew . . .

PURITY: You're joking . . .

ANNA: You've got to help me. I feel so humiliated and miserable and useless. I'm the most pathetic thing there can be in this world—a lover who gets no love. Our relationship is what priests would call "unconsummated and perverse." Even the church repudiates these unions.

PURITY: It's just a matter of time and of will.

ANNA: The good news is, he still ogles me like I'm some yummy piece of candy. When I take off my petticoat to slip on my nightgown and he sees the whiteness of my skin, his mouth just waters. But then, as if he were all gums, he can't quite sink his teeth into me. Give me your advice.

PURITY: Do you know why men like the women in bordellos? Because we're happy to get a few doubloons. Hand them over, and bing bang boom! We never ask for anything else, no love, no pleasure, no shows of affection. No orgasms, either. We only give.

ANNA: Do you mean to say that I . . . ?

PURITY: With all due respect, you have to work like you're digging for the mother lode, especially with a spent and dried-up body like His Excellency's. Fine ladies like you are too demanding. You're young and beautiful, and when you hold out your basket, wham! you're used to having it filled immediately with flowers. Men might dress you in fine clothes and hang strings of pearls around your neck or adorn your fingers with rings and your teensy ears with gems, but don't kid yourself, that's pay you're receiving. So be happy with it, and know that many of us out there are doing the same thing for a lot less. But when the moment of truth arrives . . . it's back to the mines!

ANNA: Do you believe that?

PURITY: Did you know that the Lord Secretary's wife went to her grave after thirty years of marriage without ever trotting out her little talents onstage?

ANNA: That can't be true.

PURITY: On plenty of occasions she was the one who'd call me to take her place in bed. And do you know what she would do in the meantime? Spend the day praying in the palace chapel and reading pious tracts. She was a great lady . . . no one has a bad word to say about her. But be careful! The traits people praise in a wife can be disastrous in a mistress.

ANNA: My situation is hopeless! Every day he gets skinnier, stonier, and colder . . . while that other thing just gets softer and softer.

PURITY: If you ever need me, you only have to call.

ANNA: You're very kind. *(She takes off her necklace and gives it to Purity.)* Here, this is for you.

PURITY: My lady!

ANNA: Did I mention young and full of life? If you only knew the horrible things I dream at night and how my whole body yearns for the heat of passion.

PURITY: Tell me about it! Do you think it's easy staying a virgin for my Aniceto?

ANNA: But you're a . . .

PURITY: With God knows who marching through the brothel and some guys pulling such stunts you'd think they were the devil in the flesh. Still, a girl gets by as best she can.

ANNA: Of course.

PURITY: Here's my only bit of advice: get over the worrying as much as you can, and then calmly, without mixing work and pleasure . . . bam! Get the job done!

ANNA: So you think I'll be able to . . .

PURITY: I've never known a newborn babe, no matter how tiny and soft, who, when cared for in the proper way, hasn't grown up to be a big, tall boy.

ANNA: May the Lord and Holy Virgin allow this miracle to happen!

PURITY: Permit me to kiss your hands, my lady. They can work miracles, I promise you.
(For a moment Anna regards her hands with a certain respect and moves her fingers nimbly like a pianist before a concert. Then, suddenly, the mood is broken.)

ANNA: Auntie! Auntie! Bring back that fruit you were offering from the garden.

ISABEL: Coming right up, my angel.

ANNA: My mouth has gone dry just thinking of the job ahead.

PURITY: Don't I know it, my lady.
(Isabel returns with a basket of oranges.)

ISABEL: Picked fresh from the tree.

ANNA: Here, have one. *(She takes an orange and hands another to Purity.)*

PURITY: Thank you. My mouth has gone dry, too, just mentioning those things.
(The two suck on their oranges rather lustily.)

JUAN: Give the Lord Secretary these copies, hot off the press.

BATISTA: *(Holding a leather jewel box)* Here's the jewel box with your initials carved in gold leaf.

ISABEL: Ask the Lord Secretary permission for me to embroider his coat of arms with that satin.

ANNA: *(To Vincent)* How about you? Don't you have anything to ask of me?

VINCENT: What I want the Lord Secretary won't give me.

ANNA: Who knows? He has a lot of influence. Come on, you can tell me.

VINCENT: What for?

ANNA: I'm curious.

VINCENT: I'd like to take his place in bed at night.

ANNA: *(Laughing)* Come on . . .

BATISTA: I would, too!

ISABEL: What kind of lewd talk is this? What is Purity going to think of us?

PURITY: My lady, you have to understand that in my business . . .

VINCENT: But there's a big difference between you and me, Batista. You'd be happy just switching places with him and might even thank him to boot. I, on the other hand, would love to pick him up and toss him out the bedroom window.

JUAN: That's enough bad jokes already.

ANNA: I think they're funny.

JUAN: Even so. Let's get back to the rehearsal. Anna, you can be our guest of honor.
(Anna sits in the chair, while Isabel shows her disapproval by exiting.)

JUAN: Esteemed audience, in just a few moments we will go on with the show.
(Purity and Batista take a wooden door, which will serve as a bed, and place it on a slant center stage.)

(To Vincent) I don't like you speaking so impudently. What are you trying to do, have yourself thrown into a dungeon?

VINCENT: Why in God's name are we handing over the most delectable fruit in our garden to that dried-up old prune?

JUAN: Anna is not your affair.

VINCENT: Oh no?

JUAN: Or your brother's.

VINCENT: Why not?

JUAN: Because I say so!

PURITY: Everything is ready to go.

BATISTA: Shall we proceed?

JUAN: Yes, go ahead.
(Juan and Vincent step onto the stage.)

JUAN: *(Wearing a cap with bells)* So, every night the two young kings went off to bed with their lovely serving wench.
(Purity climbs into bed as one brother lies on each side of her. She holds each one's hand after giving them both a big kiss.)

JUAN: While one satisfied his desires *(Batista cozies up to Purity)*, the other pretended to sleep. *(Vincent snores, then each does what the other has just done.)* And when the other took his pleasure, it was his cousin's turn to pretend. And so the months and years went by, with the two cousins, as the saying goes, enjoying a great "peace" together!

ANNA: *(Delighted by the scenario)* Bravo! Bravo! Well done!

ISABEL: Hush, child! Don't be improper.

ANNA: There's one wench who won't go hungry! *(She laughs)*

JUAN: But even as honey will taste sickly sweet if eaten every day, the innkeeper's daughter grew weary of all their compliments and courtly ways. . . . Here is what happened one day when a puppeteer came to town. . . .

PURITY: Oh, do a flip or two, Sir Puppeteer, and lift my sinking spirits.

JUAN: *(Speaking like a country bumpkin)* Dang! What a dainty waist and ass on this-here gal!

PURITY: A yokel after my own heart!

JUAN: You got a husbin'?

PURITY: Two, in fact, but don't worry, I'll still be yours. *(He starts taking off his breeches.)* But not just yet. Don't be impatient. I'll see you tonight.

JUAN: Now when night falls and the clock strikes twelve . . . *(Bells from a clock tower can be heard)* The young thang's luscious foot a-danglin' off the bed will be mah sahn. *(He crouches down and caresses the foot she sticks out of the bed in which the three are lying.)* Ah'm a-here!

PURITY: *(To the puppeteer)* Ooh, quit tickling! *(To Batista)* Go to sleep now, kingy, it's his turn tonight. *(To Vincent)* It's his turn tonight, kingy-ling. Just go to sleep. *(Both snore)* Come to me!

JUAN: Ah'm a-coming! *(He jumps on her but quickly reverts to being Juan Timoneda.)* Music! Music! *(Music plays, and Isabel appears unexpectedly, putting an end to the rehearsal.)*

ISABEL: Say what you will, but this kind of sleaze does not take place in Valencia.

PURITY: I have to go. It's getting dark, and men are like bats—they all come pouring out once the sun goes down. With your kind permission.

JUAN: We'll see you tomorrow.

ISABEL: Have a good one!

PURITY: Please, my lady, I'm not a pervert.

ISABEL: Forgive me, child. I didn't mean it that way. I was referring to later, after work. *(To Anna)* And where are you off to?

ANNA: To the garden, to take a walk by the orange trees.

VINCENT: I'll go with you.

ANNA: Batista is. But wait for me later in the barn. *(Just then one of her shoes falls off her foot.)* Oh, silly me! Did my shoe just fall off? Uncle, would you please slip it on for me? *(She holds out her foot coquettishly, and Juan puts her shoe back on.)* Ooh, stop tickling! Thank you, uncle dear. You've earned my eternal gratitude. *(She walks offstage laughing, holding Batista's hand.)*

PURITY: I'll try to study my lines, but they don't give me a moment. Now that spring is here, believe me, I just don't stop.

ISABEL: Poor girl.

PURITY: How would you feel about a different man knocking on your door every ten minutes?

ISABEL: Child, you forget yourself.

PURITY: Forgive me. Your fruit was delicious. God be with you all.

(Purity exits. Isabel picks up the orange peels and exits. There is a pause.)

VINCENT: Father, when you were young and in love with mother, weren't you consumed with jealousy?

JUAN: I suppose. I don't remember anymore.

(Transition)

VINCENT: Well, whenever I feel jealous I get a pain right here, like someone is jabbing me with a poker. And I hate every man who goes near her. Even though I love her, yes, I could still strangle her.

JUAN: *(Smiling)* That much in love?

VINCENT: I curse the day! You don't understand because you're old.

JUAN: Not so old I can't appreciate the charms of a young filly. . . . I have dreams sometimes, too, just like you. But over the years dreams grow shorter.

VINCENT: And when you wake up . . . ?

JUAN: I curl up into my corner of the bed and stop my ears to drown out your mother's snoring.

VINCENT: Do you fall asleep again so easily? I can't.

JUAN: At least you don't have to cover your ears.

(They both laugh.)

VINCENT: Do you ever think about the sea, father?

JUAN: Where is this question leading?

VINCENT: I do. All the time. It's so vast and smooth. You know what I like most about it? It has no roads. It's all one big road that can take you anywhere in the world.

JUAN: Or nowhere. A lot of men perish out there.

VINCENT: Bah! When I'm typesetting your stories, I envy the heroes who sail off to faraway places with the women they love, no matter how much toil and trouble lie in store for them.

JUAN: Where would you go?

VINCENT: Anyplace, just far from here.

JUAN: The day after we were married, your mother and I went down to the fisherman's quay and sat on the sand all afternoon with our feet in the water. All she could talk about was the price of fish, but I had my sights set on the horizon. I wanted to cross it and see what lay on the other side.

VINCENT: Why didn't you?

JUAN: I had just settled down and had to work for your mother and for all the children God would send us. That was the day I began writing.

VINCENT: I could never have been happy with a ream of paper and a bottle of ink. I would have crossed it then and there.

JUAN: Well, you would have been disappointed because there is no horizon or line or anything out there. It's all a trick our eyes play on us. No matter how long you sail, some unreachable beyond will always be sitting out there before you.

VINCENT: I'll reach it some day, no matter how far it is.

JUAN: That's a pipe dream.

   (Pause)

VINCENT: Would you have the guts to come with me, father?

JUAN: Me?

VINCENT: The two of us together, like old friends. Don't tell me the idea doesn't appeal to you.

JUAN: Then I won't. But that's just not possible.

VINCENT: Why not? Wouldn't you like to reach the impossible with me?

JUAN: You're crazy.

(Pause)

VINCENT: You still haven't answered me.

JUAN: All right, then, yes. Yes, I would like that. To tell you the truth, I've spent my whole life intending to without even once getting up from my chair.

(Pause. The two might embrace, or Juan might put his hand on his son's shoulder. Purity suddenly bursts in from the street.)

PURITY: There's big news from the court! I came as fast as I could to tell you.

JUAN: What's happening?

PURITY: Well, I was late getting back to the brothel, so I rushed upstairs to my room to put on, or maybe I should say take off, my work clothes. But when I went downstairs to the parlor, whom do you think I should see there? Nobody! Just the other working girls, not a single man. It looks like the news has spread like wildfire through Valencia, and everyone knows.

JUAN: Knows what?

PURITY: Since we cater to such a distinguished clientele—all very important people, officials, dignitaries, clergymen from the cathedral—of course, they'd be the first to hear. May I sit down? *(She sits)* I'm so overheated I need to catch my breath.

ISABEL: *(Entering)* What's this woman doing here?

PURITY: I've come to bring you the news. Oh my lady, all the things that are happening, I just can't believe it.

ISABEL: What is it? Oh, do tell . . .

PURITY: Well, this afternoon . . .

ISABEL: *(To Vincent, who shows no interest and gets up to leave)* Hey, where are you going?

VINCENT: To the barn.

ISABEL: What for?

VINCENT: To tend to . . . the animals. *(Vincent exits)*

ISABEL: At this hour? *(To Purity)* You were saying . . .

PURITY: Well, this afternoon . . .

(Batista enters)

ISABEL: And where have you been?

BATISTA: In the garden.

ISABEL: And what were you doing in the garden?

BATISTA: Eating oranges with Anna. I had two . . . almost three! Mother, those oranges are delicious! Oh, mother! *(He collapses in a chair, spent.)*

ISABEL: I don't understand a thing that's going on here.

PURITY: So, should I tell you the news or not? Because if you aren't going to pay attention, I'm leaving.

ISABEL: I've been asking you to tell me for the longest time now.

PURITY: Well, this afternoon the Lord Patriarch shows up at the Vicereine's palace with a crucifix in his hand and sets the poor lady straight about a thing or two.

ISABEL: Mary, mother of God!

PURITY: It turns out that Valencia is practically Sodom and Gomorrah and that any day now the Lord above will burn us all to a crisp with the fire of His justice.

ISABEL: That's ridiculous! I'm not saying there are no sinners here—every place has its share of them. But we hold processions every month in honor of the widest variety of saints, and the city itself is under the protection of the Blessed Virgin of the Downtrodden.

PURITY: Well, from the sounds of it, that's not enough.

JUAN: How did the Vicereine respond?

PURITY: That's the worst part. As soon as the poor gal heard this, she started to feel queasy, and they had to loosen her skirt and give her smelling salts.

ISABEL: And the Patriarch?

PURITY: The same as ever, carrying on about how the women here have no shame and sleep with whomever they like, about how officials steal and priests go on binges with the money they collect from alms and bulls. . . . You know, the usual.

ISABEL: This is an insult to all decent people.

PURITY: And a lie. Do I sleep with whomever strikes my fancy? No ma'am, only with my clients. How about you? Do you sleep with whomever you wish?

ISABEL: Please, child, don't compare me to . . .

PURITY: Then he goes rattling off the books he claims are wicked and the plays and paintings, too. And that Luber or Luther guy, whatever his name is, really put him in a snit! You'd think the man was the devil incarnate.

ISABEL: What have you to say about all this? You haven't uttered a word yet.

JUAN: I expected something of the sort. I just didn't think it would happen so soon.

ISABEL: You knew about this?

JUAN: Winds of fanaticism are blowing across all of Europe. The fear that Protestantism and other evils might reach here from abroad is sure to bring severe repression. I'm afraid we've seen the last of writers from Italy or any other country that ever showed us the joy of living.

PURITY: Wait, there's more. The person accompanying the Patriarch and seconding everything he said was none other than our own Lord Secretary! Maybe this newfound passion will make him stiff once and for all!

ISABEL: You mean, our Anna's gentleman?

PURITY: One and the same. Either I'm mistaken, or your niece's days at the palace are numbered.

ISABEL: Oh God, what a terrible setback for the child! And just when her future was looking so bright.

PURITY: My lady, there's no place like bed for getting to know a guy. I speak from experience: never trust a man who, when the time comes, doesn't shoot his load immediately. The more trouble he has, the less he's to be trusted.

ISABEL: Do you mean to say that the Lord Secretary is . . .

PURITY: A limpdick!

ISABEL: *(Making the sign of the cross)* Heaven help us all!
(Anna enters looking extremely happy, with orange blossoms in one hand and a straw basket in the other.)

ANNA: Oh, auntie, I'm so happy. . . . It's been really wonderful seeing the old house again.

ISABEL: *(Giving her a hug)* My poor darling child. . . . Don't you worry, there will always be a place for you here, whatever comes to pass.

ANNA: And what is coming to pass?

JUAN: We all love you dearly, Anna.

ANNA: *(To Juan)* You, too?

JUAN: Of course, girl.

ANNA: *(Giving him a hug)* Then I have everything I need to make me completely happy. *(She kisses him and sits down.)*

PURITY: If that mean old shriveled-up prune is going to play the poor thing this way, I swear on my love for my Aniceto, he can find someone else to float his boat!
(Vincent enters, sighing with satisfaction and holding a sheaf of hay. He sits down beside his printing presses, happy and exhausted, so now Vincent, Batista, and Anna are all seated and looking spent. Purity exits.
The bell at the front gate rings, and Purity enters again.)

PURITY: Oh my lady, it's . . . limpdick!

JUAN: Let me speak with him alone. You go, too, Anna, and bring some torches to light the courtyard.

(Anna, Vincent, and Batista exit with Purity.)

ISABEL: He's stepping out of his carriage with a real hangdog look on his face!

(The bell rings again.)

JUAN: *(To Isabel)* Go let him in.

(Isabel exits and returns with the Lord Secretary, who is dressed rather austerely in contrast to the way he appeared in the previous act.)

JUAN: Excellency . . .

ISABEL: Shall I bring out a jug of wine?

SECRETARY: I never drink.

ISABEL: Since when?

SECRETARY: Since I became so inclined.

ISABEL: Some fruit, perhaps?

SECRETARY: The days of wine and roses are over. This city will return to being the mirror of virtue and fine manners it was in the past.

ISABEL: May I at least bring out a torch so you'll have some light? Or is it considered fine manners to sit in the dark like owls and go bumping into walls?

SECRETARY: Yes, bring us some light, that it may illuminate our souls.

ISABEL: And our walls.

(The light indeed is low, as it is almost night. The rest of the house is dark. Isabel exits and returns a short while later with a torch to light the front yard.)

SECRETARY: I've always considered you a reasonable man, Juan, loyal to the interests of the realm and smart enough to know what is good for you.

JUAN: *(Vague)* That's very kind of you, Excellency . . .

ISABEL: *(Entering)* A flame for expunging mosquitoes and sins! *(She places the torch in a holder and lingers with no intention of leaving.)*

JUAN: Isabel, you probably have some chores to do.

ISABEL: No, not a one.

SECRETARY: I wouldn't wish to keep you from your housework.

ISABEL: What are you talking about? You never keep me from anything! *(Giving him some hearty slaps on the back)* In a way, you're like one of the family!

SECRETARY: *(Cross)* But only in a way.

JUAN: *(Making one final attempt to get her to leave)* Isabel, don't you think . . .

ISABEL: *(Pulling up a chair and sitting beside them)* No, I don't. Come now, let's get on with it. I'm not going anywhere. *(The men look at each other in resignation.)*

JUAN: Fine, just keep your mouth shut.

ISABEL: Not a word. Tick-a-lock.

SECRETARY: I suppose you have heard about what occurred at the palace this afternoon.

JUAN: There are rumors to the effect that . . .

ISABEL: It must have been horrible for you, especially in light of your high esteem for the Vicereine.

SECRETARY: You cannot begin to imagine.

ISABEL: At the very least, for allowing you to install our Anna in your bed.

SECRETARY: That is precisely one of the matters I have come to discuss.

JUAN: Mother of God, Isabel! Shut up for once in your life and let the Lord Secretary speak!

SECRETARY: The paths of Providence are inscrutable and often difficult for man to understand. In this instance, however, the pious words of the Patriarch and the Vicereine's demise have made the Supreme Will abundantly clear.

JUAN: What did you say? Our Lady is dead?

SECRETARY: The symptoms she shows are quite serious, indeed. It appears to be only a matter of hours, perhaps even minutes.

ISABEL: God, what a terrible misfortune!

SECRETARY: We must accept the ways of the Lord joyfully.

ISABEL: Are you going to rejoice when Our Lady buys the farm?

SECRETARY: The Patriarch himself has heard her confession, and she has been given extreme unction. All the palace clergy are saying one prayer after another for the dead. In heaven above the angels impatiently wait to escort her purified soul to the mansion of Our Lord.

ISABEL: Her mansion down here isn't too shabby, either. It's the finest in all Valencia.

JUAN: What will become of the realm?

SECRETARY: We shall have to save it from going all to . . . perdition.

ISABEL: Jesus! I had no idea.

SECRETARY: And if battling sin and vice in this deluded land of ours should mean erecting once again the gallows that served us so well during the artisan rebellion, then I say "hang them high," and that is that. Don't you agree?

JUAN: I don't understand politics. *(To Isabel, who was about to protest)* And you be quiet!

SECRETARY: A sinner swinging from the end of a rope loses all desire to succumb to vice.

ISABEL: Or to virtue, Excellency.

SECRETARY: The Lord Patriarch has honored me by placing in my charge the noble fight against Protestant heresy.

JUAN: But Your Lordship, there have never been any Protestants here.

SECRETARY: Well, some may show up. Now, as for women, we must see to it that they dress with proper modesty.

ISABEL: Good God, do you intend to pick our nightgowns for us?

SECRETARY: As St. Jerome said: the devil avails himself of female forms to lead men into lechery.

ISABEL: Look, Excellency, no matter how hard you try, you'll never turn women into dried-up, leathery-skinned horrors like yourself!

JUAN: That's enough stupid talk, Isabel. Leave us alone now.

ISABEL: Fine, I'm going. But if we women didn't bring a little spice to this place, the whole population of Valencia would disappear like that. *(Exit)*

JUAN: Please excuse her . . .

SECRETARY: Women are ambassadors from hell. Do as I do, Juan: keep chaste. But let us turn now to the reason for my visit: the theatrical piece you are writing for the festival.

JUAN: We're still working on it.

SECRETARY: It will have to be replaced.

JUAN: What? The Vicereine herself chose that play.

SECRETARY: Forget about the Vicereine and write some other drama that won't scandalize honest folk with its excesses.

JUAN: That's just not possible, there isn't time.

SECRETARY: You have more than enough talent to come up with a piece that will move us all to piety and reflection. This year I want the Festival of the Holy Blood to be one of extreme penitence, fervor, and prayer. More festive than ever!

JUAN: I see.

SECRETARY: That is the wish of the brotherhood, in which, by the way, your membership, for the moment, will just not be possible.

JUAN: But you assured me that . . .

SECRETARY: Everyone knows a woman from your family was living scandalously as a concubine to a gentleman of the court.

JUAN: Yes, you!

SECRETARY: Whomever. You will also have to burn these immoral leaflets you publish.

JUAN: But they're only stories to amuse the public.

SECRETARY: Amusement is the mother of all vices.

JUAN: What am I supposed to print, then?

SECRETARY: The lives of saints, novenas, Bibles . . . no, not the Bible, that book is too dangerous.

JUAN: But no one is going to buy those things.

SECRETARY: You are mistaken. People accept what they are given and end up needing it like sustenance itself. Don't be fooled, Juan. You don't publish what people want; people end up wanting what you publish.

JUAN: You place too high a value on my work, Excellency.

SECRETARY: In the future, whoever possesses the printing press or some such invention will control the world.

JUAN: But the powers that be will always control the press.

SECRETARY: Let us just say that you, with your talent and calling, are the lever, and I . . . the fulcrum you need to lift the world. Any world.

JUAN: Like the one the Lord Patriarch is trying to impose?

SECRETARY: The Lord Patriarch, the Pope, the King, and the Council of Trent. . . . And now I must ask you for a personal favor. It would be best for now that your niece, Anna, stay with you here. I, as well as the powers above me, would look most favorably upon her entering a convent.

JUAN: You can't force her to do that.

SECRETARY: Moreover, let me make it clear that I am returning her precisely as I found her. Just between you and me, the girl is somewhat clumsy in bed, so I don't owe you a thing. And that is that.

ISABEL: *(Entering with Anna)* What do you mean, "That is that"? You bag of bones! You impotent old pig!

JUAN: Isabel, watch your mouth!

ISABEL: What about all that pinching? The girl's bottom is purpler than a priest's robe during Lent!

SECRETARY: My good woman!

ISABEL: Go on, child, show your uncle your ass.

JUAN: For Christ's sake, Isabel!

ISABEL: Returning her just as you found her, eh? Don't owe us a thing, eh?

SECRETARY: Not a thing.

ISABEL: Well, it's not from a lack of trying! The poor girl did all she could to satisfy your whims.

ANNA: Every last one of them, auntie.

ISABEL: It's because you've got a pecker that's deader than Lazarus, although Christ himself couldn't make that thing rise again.

JUAN: That's enough!

SECRETARY: The mother superior of the Sisters who Adore St. Philomena of Antioch has agreed to accept you as a novice at her convent. She is expecting you tomorrow morning. At ten. Do be punctual so as not to interrupt her hour of prayer. As for the dowry, I will see that it is distributed to the community.

ISABEL: I don't give a rap about your dowry, the mother superior, the community, or all the Philomenas in Antioch!

SECRETARY: May the Lord forgive your sins as I do. God be with you all. *(Exit)*

ISABEL: You rotten, impotent dog!

ANNA: But I don't want to be a nun. I'll whore with Purity first!

ISABEL: I'll go with you. We'll both be whores! Oh, the things that man makes me say!
(Anna rushes offstage in tears, passing Batista and Vincent, who perk up and are surprised by their cousin's rage.)

BATISTA: What's wrong with Anna?

VINCENT: What's happening?

JUAN: Exactly what we deserve. Shit. Shit, shit, shit!!!

VINCENT: Father!

BATISTA: Father, what is it?

ISABEL: Holy Mary! *(To Batista)* There's a small flask of whiskey and herbs in the pantry. Bring it here. *(Batista obeys. To Vincent)* And you, go get a doctor.

JUAN: No!

ISABEL: You're not well, Juan. I've never seen you like this before. *(Giving him the concoction their son has brought)* Here, drink some of this, swallow it slowly. . . . Now take deep breaths, that's it. . . . Calm down. . . .

VINCENT: What happened?

ISABEL: The Lord Secretary came and ordered Anna out of his palace.

BATISTA: *(Happy)* Then she's staying with us?

ISABEL: She is to take her vows in a convent tomorrow.

VINCENT: No!

JUAN: Until today they only asked us to be their jesters. Now they want every-thing—my press, my books, my talent . . . even all of you.

BATISTA: Perhaps if you handle this matter delicately, we'll come out with even more privilege than we had before.

VINCENT: You're not going to stand for this?

ISABEL: No, boys, he is not, I assure you. He'll never grovel before those nobodies again.

JUAN: That's just . . .

ISABEL: We won't let you. Aren't you the most clever, handsome man in Spain?

JUAN: What does that have to do with anything?

ISABEL: You've swallowed your pride before to make these nonentities forgive you for your talent. But this time they've gone too far, and you'll have to pluck up your courage and tell them we are not for sale.

JUAN: Don't be naive, Isabel. They can buy whatever or whomever they want.

ISABEL: But not you.

JUAN: My rebel laundress. What are you proposing, another artisan uprising? Don't forget, they hanged every last insurgent.

ISABEL: But on their feet and unbowed.

BATISTA: You're splitting hairs, mother.

JUAN: What can I do?

ISABEL: Burn the machines, tear down the house, sow the garden with salt.

JUAN: Then what?

ISABEL: Cut off your head if you have to, but never hand them your talent.

BATISTA: You're talking nonsense, mother.

VINCENT: Or clear out of here. It's a big world out there.

BATISTA: What, and leave all this behind? Let them stew in their politicking and squabbles. We have our own lives to lead here with the shop, our profession ...

VINCENT: Our humiliation.

BATISTA: That may be! But we're getting ahead, and that's what counts.

VINCENT: But what about Anna?

BATISTA: She's better off in a convent than in that old pervert's clutches.

VINCENT: You're a lousy bastard!

BATISTA: And you're a jerk!

JUAN: That's enough! *(To Isabel)* How is dinner coming along?

ISABEL: I've put the rice on the fire. It'll be ready soon.

JUAN: You know what they say: "Good food and a drink will help you to think."

VINCENT: Are you going to do their bidding? Have you no pride?

JUAN: I have my pride ... and my fear and my profession and my family. So many things, too many things are buzzing around in my head for me to have any peace right now.

VINCENT: With all your talent, do you know why you're not the most famous writer in the world? Because at the slightest sign of trouble you shit in your pants.

JUAN: Supper, everyone!

ISABEL: Aren't you coming?

JUAN: I'm not hungry. . . . I'm going to spend the night here. I've been commanded to write a new play for the Festival of the Holy Blood.

VINCENT: You're not going to oblige them?

JUAN: I may write one, or, quite the opposite, I may just decide to take your mother's advice and start another artisan rebellion. That way I can become the most famous writer in the world ever to hang from a rope. Leave me alone now, I beg you.

ISABEL: Come.

(Isabel, Batista, and Vincent exit. Juan picks up the pen he has been using and throws it to the ground. He approaches the stage platform on which the script of the play lies, looks at it, and tears it to pieces. Anna enters.)

ANNA: I feel so destitute! When I think that I may never see auntie or my cousins or you again . . .

JUAN: Anna . . .

ANNA: Can I step on the stage? No one should object, since that pig of a Court Secretary is not my lord and master anymore.

JUAN: Of course.

ANNA: I'll come out ahead in one respect . . . at least I won't have to sleep with him anymore. *(Sitting on the platform meant to represent the bed)* Ah, the lovers' bed in your farce. *(Leaving her legs provocatively exposed)*

JUAN: Cover yourself up!

ANNA: *(Disregarding him)* I was waiting for you in my room.

JUAN: I already told you that will never happen again.

ANNA: Not even tonight? Can't you see I'm even more miserable now than I was then? This time it's not just a bad dream.

JUAN: You poor girl.

ANNA: Put your arms around me. I want to forget for just a moment what lies ahead for me.

JUAN: *(With the two of them in an embrace)* Anna . . .

ANNA: You're miserable tonight, too. Let my body console you, and you won't feel so sad.

JUAN: *(Burying his head in her breast)* My God . . .

ANNA: We're both so sad.
   (They kiss. Vincent enters.)

VINCENT: I can't believe it! You and my father!

ANNA: What's it to you?

VINCENT: You're a tart! A floozy . . . a whore!

JUAN: I forbid you to insult her.

VINCENT: You can't forbid me to do anything from now on.

ANNA: What kind of son are you to feel that way just because I give your father a little kiss?

VINCENT: So everything you told me was a lie?

ANNA: No, but that has nothing to do with this. You're the one I love.

VINCENT: Come off it!

ANNA: But I love him, too.

VINCENT: Men are all the same to you. You see, father? She's no better than a bitch in heat, a cunning little vixen!

ANNA: And you're a vulgar bully!

JUAN: Stop shouting, both of you! You'll disturb the whole house.

VINCENT: I'm going to give you such a . . .

ANNA: You wouldn't dare, you coward!

JUAN: That's enough! Be quiet! Enough!

(Isabel enters)

ISABEL: What's all this screaming about?

JUAN: Nothing, Isabel, just the kids quarreling.

VINCENT: It's private, mother.

ISABEL: Don't you know, you hopeless case, that I'm aware of everything that goes on in this house?

JUAN: Isabel, I think that . . .

ISABEL: And you . . . you're more hopeless than your son. It's just as well that you have me around to impose a little order in this family.

BATISTA: *(Entering)* What's going on, mother?

ISABEL: Just what we needed! Not a peep out of you, understand? Vincent, come here and give your mother a hug. Or were you planning to leave without saying goodbye?

VINCENT: How did you know?

ISABEL: I saw the bag you packed with your things. I threw in a few gold coins for the trip.

JUAN: What trip?

VINCENT: I'm going away, father, to the quay. Setting sail on the first ship out of here, no matter where it's headed.

ISABEL: I packed Anna's clothes, too.

JUAN: What are you up to, woman?

ISABEL: Well, if Vincent is going, he should take Anna with him.

VINCENT: Her? Wild horses couldn't drag me anywhere with that tart!

ISABEL: Don't you think the poor girl deserves a better fate than the one in store for her here?

VINCENT: What's it to me?

ISABEL: Are you so cruel that you'd sentence her to life in a convent because of your ridiculous jealousy?

VINCENT: You don't know what she's done to me.

ISABEL: Silly boy, don't you see that you're the guy who is getting the girl in the end?

BATISTA: Hey, how come Vincent gets her and not me?

ISABEL: Because you're shrewder, and you don't want to give up the shop.

BATISTA: Well, when you put it that way . . .

ISABEL: Juan Timoneda, give your blessing and a big fatherly hug . . . to both of them.

VINCENT: *(Embracing Juan reluctantly)* I'm only doing this for mother because if it were up to me . . .

ANNA: *(Embracing Juan)* I'll never forget you . . .

JUAN: He'll make you forget.

ANNA: Never. I'll always love you.

JUAN: I don't believe you . . . but thank you anyway.

ISABEL: Go on already, or you won't get there in time. The ships leave port at dawn.

VINCENT: I'm not going!

ANNA: I'll take the convent over this!

ISABEL: Juan, you're master of the house. Wield some authority.

VINCENT: I'll have you know I won't say a word to this floozy for the rest of my life!

ANNA: That goes for me with this lout, too!

JUAN: For the love of God, be off, the two of you, once and for all!

ANNA and VINCENT: *(Shouting at the same time)* Ruffian! Who do you think you are? I'm offended! I'm the one who should be offended! You! etc., etc . . . *(Juan watches as the couple exits)*

JUAN: I have a lot to do: tear down the house, sow the garden with salt, set the machinery on fire so that everything—and I mean everything—burns. . . . Maybe even cut off my own head.

BATISTA: You're talking nonsense, father. *(Juan picks up the torch and sets the stage curtains on fire.)*

ISABEL: What are you doing?

JUAN: I've been ordered to destroy all the books and leaflets we've printed, but they can't expect me just to hand them the place where all my hopes and dreams abide.

BATISTA: Have you lost your mind? The fire will spread to the house!

ISABEL: Do you know you look more handsome than ever tonight?

JUAN: You look like a girl again, Isabel.

BATISTA: Aren't you going to help me? My God, the two of them have gone insane! Help! Water! Water!

ISABEL: Do you love me, Juan?

JUAN: In my eyes you're still the loveliest laundress in all Valencia.

ISABEL: And in mine you're the best guy in the world. *(They hug while Batista tries to extinguish the flames with a blanket.)*

JUAN: Dignity or ruin. They leave us no other choice.

ISABEL: Can we afford aspiring to dignity if it means reducing an honorable life to ashes?

JUAN: *(Shrugging his shoulders)* Go on, help your son put out the fire. *(To Batista)* And you, tell the neighbors to bring some water from the ditch.

BATISTA: Aren't you going to do anything?

JUAN: I'm about to write the new work for the festival in honor of the city's principal personages. Our little farce should enhance their piety and devotion so the whole town will praise their virtue and holiness. . . . So be it.

(All at once the flames go out and the action stops. Juan puts on two large horns and speaks to the audience.)

Why must this world put on parade
A throng of man and womankind
The slightest scrutiny would find
If not betrayers, then betrayed?
The horns duped lovers sprout reflect
A far less knavish treachery
Than those of rogues who genuflect
To bishops and nobility.
This growth of horns thus proves fair price
For future riches to be gained.
God bless, kind folks, you've been too nice.
Applaud if you leave entertained.

CURTAIN

(When taking their bows, all the actors wear horns except for Vincent and Anna, who are rowing a clunky boat.)

SONG

ALL: And so our horny cuckolds' song
    Resounds with joy through dell and mew.
    We proudly sport these signs of wrong
    In sly contentment all day long—
    What else is there for us to do?
    Our wearing horns is evidence
    That pandering is easy fare.
    Be blind and mute in all events
    Act like a fish, ignore good sense
    And swim the sea without a care.
    Two types of cuckolds may be found:
    Those doomed by spouses or by deed.
    For once you give these pimps some ground
    And lend them something honor-bound,
    They're sure to screw you—that's their creed.
    A king possesses potent charms—

Cuckolding you is one of these.
The prize for suffering such harms
Is medals and a coat of arms
To suit a baron or marquise.
And so our horny cuckolds' song
Resounds with joy through dell and mew.
We proudly sport these signs of wrong
In sly contentment all day long—
What else is there for us to do?

The Other William

(*EL OTRO WILLIAM*)

by Jaime Salom

Translated by Phyllis Zatlin

Characters

WILLIAM

WILLIAM SHAKESPEARE

COSTRAND

THE JUDGE

MARY

DOWAGER COUNTESS, widow of the Fifth Earl of Derby

LADY DERBY, wife of the Sixth Earl of Derby

Act 1

SCENE

Library, in Chester Castle. An entrance door. At the rear, a large window overlooking the gardens. A table, with a bottle of water and glasses, a tape recorder, old books, and a human skull. The bookcases can be opened like doors to allow characters to enter and exit as indicated. The real door will be used only at the beginning and end of the play.

(Enter WILLIAM. *He is wearing a tour guide's cap.)*

WILLIAM: This way, ladies and gentlemen, come along. Is everyone here? Good. Now that we've toured the courtyard, the great halls, the kitchens, and the earls' private quarters, we shall finish our visit of the castle in this charming library. This is the most interesting part of our tour, so I shall give a somewhat longer explanation. Please have a seat. Madam, there's a chair over there. Good. We are now in the most secluded part of the building: the sanctum sanctorum of the Sixth Earl of Derby, the most famous member of his house. On his mother's side, he was descended from the royal family and was considered one of the possible pretenders to the throne, to succeed Queen Elizabeth. But he avoided political intrigue and devoted most of his life to writing. Right here, at this cedar table. Carved by Scottish artisans, it was a present from King Henry VII to the First Earl of Derby, in appreciation for his heroic actions at the Battle of Bosworth Field. Excuse me, sir, but no smoking is allowed. You'll have to wait until we go out to the gardens. Thank you. *(He picks up a book.)* I'm holding a manuscript that recounts amazing events in this family's history. It is in the Earl's own handwriting—even if some critics deny its authenticity. "The Life and Deeds of Sir William Stanley, Sixth Earl of Derby." Yes, madam? Of course you may ask a question. The skull? Apparently, it's been on this table since the Earl's time. They say it was Yorick's skull, a family jester, but no one knows for sure. *(He plays music on the tape recorder and opens the book.)*

Dawn, on a spring morning in the sixteenth century.

(A bookcase slides open. Enter Costrand, a servant to the Stanley family. He is dressed in a period costume and is carrying an elegant tray of food, which he leaves on the table. William has removed his cap.)

COSTRAND: Good morning, my lord.

WILLIAM: *(Reading)* Accursèd rascal! Have the servants in this palace forgotten that at the break of day, when the roosters crow and the lambs bleat, their master sits down at this table to take the repast commonly referred to as breakfast?

COSTRAND: Please forgive your humble servant's tardiness.

WILLIAM: *(To his listeners)* Don't be surprised by the high-flown speech. Back then, that was my usual way of expressing myself. *(To Costrand)* You're late, you laggard. Long since the day stood tiptoe on the misty mountaintops. I hear the lark, the herald of the morn.

COSTRAND: It's the nightingale and not the lark that caresses your ear. Every night she sings in yon pomegranate tree. Believe me, sir, it's the nightingale.

WILLIAM: *(No longer reading)* You dare contradict your master? And what do you think you'll get for such cheek? Shall I have you flogged again, like last week? *(To his listeners)* In those days that's the way masters treated their servants. The more lordly the masters, the more brutish. *(To Costrand)* What, no fruit?

COSTRAND: Your servant, Mary, has gone to the garden to pick some fresh from the tree. Here she comes.

(Mary enters, carrying a basket of fruit.)

MARY: *(Sitting on William's lap)* There are still drops of dew on their peel the way my beloved lord likes them.

WILLIAM: Dear daughter of Eve, who brings me an apple every dawn.

MARY: *(Naughtily)* So that you can bite its juicy flesh.
(William bites the apple. Costrand views the scene, fascinated. William becomes aware of his continued presence.)

WILLIAM: What are you looking at? Get out or I'll kick you out.

COSTRAND: *(Quickly exiting)* Yes, your lordship.

MARY: *(Putting a strawberry in his mouth)* A strawberry for my darling bunny, my precious white dove. . . . And a caress for my dear mouse's mischievous tail. *(She caresses him between the legs.)* Would you like me to get undressed?

WILLIAM: This isn't the right time.

MARY: From what I can feel, I'd say it was.

WILLIAM: Tonight.

MARY: *(Coquettish)* Night is many hours away. . . . Your administrators await in the outer chamber to present you with the accounts.

WILLIAM: Let them take their damned accounts and leave me be! I have more important things to do than attend to that pack of thieves. Tell them to give the money to Costrand and go away.

MARY: As you command, my lord.

WILLIAM: By the way, do you like that rascal?

MARY: Who, Costrand? What ideas you get in your head!

WILLIAM: Well, his eyes pop out whenever he looks at you. Someday, if you continue to serve me well, I'll let you marry him. But until then, whether you like it or not, you have to be faithful to me.

MARY: Don't talk like that. It makes me sad. You know full well that I am only happy when I give pleasure to my master.
(She throws him a kiss and exits.)

WILLIAM: *(To his listeners)* In those days women faded fast. No sooner did they turn twenty-five than they caught smallpox or their teeth fell out. So after one used them, one disposed of them properly. By marrying them off to some yokel.
(Enter Costrand, followed by Mary, carrying a luxurious doublet.)

COSTRAND: Hail to thee, Earl of Derby! *(Kneeling)* I bend my knee before your lordship.

WILLIAM: Have you gone mad, dammit? I'm not an Earl.

COSTRAND: Yes you are, my gracious lord. That is the news I bring. Your brother died suddenly last night. Because he had no male offspring, the title is yours. I kneel before our good lord, the Sixth Earl of Derby. May God bless and keep you many years.

MARY: *(Kneeling)* Long live our noble lord, the Earl!

WILLIAM: Get up.

(Costrand and Mary assist him in putting on the doublet.)

COSTRAND: All the servants in the castle are enraptured over the news. There is much singing and dancing. They've burst into the kitchen and are stuffing their faces. They've opened the taps on the casks in the wine cellar.

WILLIAM: No one on my estate will celebrate the death of my beloved brother. Get out! Leave me alone!

COSTRAND: *(Bowing his way to the exit)* Your lordship.

MARY: Until tonight, my lord.

WILLIAM: No, my precious. Tonight, out of respect for the deceased, we shall abstain.

(Exit Mary)

WILLIAM: *(To his listeners)* That was how I found out I was an earl. Marvelous news! For the County of Derby carried with it endless benefits, lands, and flocks. To be sure, being an earl carries its dangers, too. Maybe they poisoned my poor brother; it wouldn't be the first case of that. Maybe he was murdered by Catholics who could not forgive his loyalty to an Anglican Queen. Well, may he rest in peace. Just as long as they don't try to involve me in their intrigues and they let me write. Because, first and foremost, I'm a writer. And, I don't mind saying it myself, a great writer, even though writing's looked down upon by this hypocritical society. They think of writers as little more than jesters, a real disgrace for anyone belonging to one of the noble families of the kingdom. And if one's an earl, well, unthinkable! At the moment I've got a new work going through my head. A little play about a couple of youngsters who fall in love but whose parents oppose their marriage. I'm going to call it Romualdo and Juslinda. Or maybe Romeo and Juliet. We can decide that later.

(Enter Costrand)

COSTRAND: My lady the Dowager Countess of Derby requests that your lordship receive her.

WILLIAM: My sister-in-law! What is that witch doing here? *(To Costrand)* See her in.

(Exit Costrand)

She's a fearsome woman, more dangerous than a viper. I'd a thousand times rather fend off a fever than have to put up with that harpy.

(Enter the Dowager Countess)

DOWAGER: My beloved William . . .

WILLIAM: My dearest sister-in-law.

DOWAGER: Since my good husband lies beneath the ground, my eyes are overcome with tears, and my body is but a fragile ship on a sea of sadness.

WILLIAM: My sorrow is as heartrending as yours.

DOWAGER: The genius of his life, buried under a cruel stone.

WILLIAM: He was a great man.

DOWAGER: Rather irritable and stubborn, to be sure, but a great man.

WILLIAM: A sad loss.

DOWAGER: For which I shall never be consoled. But let us momentarily forget our grief and concern ourselves with the provisions of the will your noble brother made before dying.

WILLIAM: What say you? My brother made a will?

DOWAGER: He made a will.

WILLIAM: He had no right to do that. The estate that he controlled for life belonged not to him but to the County of Derby.

DOWAGER: The title is yours in that God willed it so, and no human decision can change that. But all the rest—the castles, the land, the forests, and the flocks—he bequeathed to me and to my daughters.

WILLIAM: You are suggesting that he disinherited me?

DOWAGER: So attests the parchment, which I keep in a coffer under seven locks
. . . so no one might be tempted to snatch it from me. In short, of the legacy
you will see not a pound.

WILLIAM: He had no right to do that!

DOWAGER: No one can prevent a husband from protecting his wife and young
daughters. You well know how much he loved me.

WILLIAM: You always fought like cats and dogs! You had to close the windows and
doors to keep others from hearing your constant screaming and yelling.

DOWAGER: That's a lie.

WILLIAM: I heard you many times with my own ears.

DOWAGER: Then your ears deceived you. Our home was always a tranquil refuge of
peace and harmony. Now it is true that your brother had a devilish temperament, like all noble lords, and a loud, authoritarian voice. But I, with
my sweet, feminine ways, always smoothed over his obnoxious remarks.

WILLIAM: You're the one who convinced my brother to commit this treachery.
No one, in all the history of the Derbys, has ever so threatened the integrity
of the county.

DOWAGER: It was your neglect of your properties that moved him to act in this
manner!

WILLIAM: I don't understand.

DOWAGER: Just look at the deplorable condition of your estate, even of this castle.
As your noble brother would say, you've turned it into a dung heap.

WILLIAM: My brother would never say such an uncouth thing.

DOWAGER: Then I will. Your fields have gone to weed, the castle halls are dirty,
garbage is piled up in your kitchens, the tapestries are unraveling, and your
table *(passing her finger over it)* is covered with dust and the most bizarre
objects.
*(She picks up the skull, looks at it horrified, sets it back down, and then supersti-
tiously knocks on the wooden table.)*

WILLIAM: But the title carries unavoidable responsibilities! Maintaining an army for the Queen, feeding the people, repairing roads and bridges. How can I maintain my dignity as an earl if my brother raises his worm-eaten arms to strangle me from the grave?

DOWAGER: Use your own estate.

WILLIAM: My coffers are empty, my lands are poor, my livestock few in number.

DOWAGER: Well, you'll just have to make do.

WILLIAM: This is robbery, madam. Just as base as if bandits assaulted travelers and left their victims on the road bare-assed.

DOWAGER: Don't be crude.

WILLIAM: But you have left me as naked as they!

DOWAGER: Well then, find yourself a money lender. I've heard about a Jew named Shylock who has made a fortune lending large sums to noblemen.

WILLIAM: And how would I repay the loan? Cut off a pound of my fair flesh and hand it to him as a forfeit?

DOWAGER: There's no need to be melodramatic. Together, you and I can find a solution to your problems.

WILLIAM: I don't trust your solutions.

DOWAGER: You possess a quality, quite rare for someone your age, that can benefit you greatly.

WILLIAM: I don't see how my writing can help me.

DOWAGER: I don't mean that. You're a bachelor. Marry a wealthy lady.

WILLIAM: Who would marry a ruined earl?

DOWAGER: Don't underestimate yourself. You're still a strong man, a bit short perhaps, but when you stand up straight you do have a proud bearing. Forgive my boldness, but you are rather handsome. In that respect, you don't resemble your brother. My poor husband had his good points, but ugly . . . he was ugly, downright ugly. With bad breath and hairs growing out his ears.

WILLIAM: In battle, his was the most daring sword in all the army.

DOWAGER: But after he married, the only battles he fought were in our home. His sword now lies next to his dead body, one hopes for all eternity. *(Feeling obliged to cry at the memory)* Forgive me if tears flood my eyes.

WILLIAM: Do you really think I might still inspire love in a young lady?

DOWAGER: Why should she have to be young? You're no longer a child. And at every age we women retain qualities that are capable of satisfying even the most demanding of men. Turn your eyes toward me, in all sincerity. Does it seem to you that mourning has detracted from my charms?

WILLIAM: Well, no . . . I suppose not . . .

DOWAGER: And that my body is less desirable just because I'm a widow?

WILLIAM: *(Ambiguously)* You always were an amazing lady.

DOWAGER: For you, too? *(Modestly)* Oh, don't look at me like that and make me blush.

WILLIAM: You are the one who invited me to do so.

DOWAGER: So you would realize that your situation can easily be resolved.

WILLIAM: What are you getting at?

DOWAGER: When a tree has been split into two branches, one can unite those two branches *(putting her hands together)* to form once again the common trunk.

WILLIAM: I don't understand.

DOWAGER: Imagine for a moment that you are a branch, an illustrious branch. And I am a sweet little branch, with green, swaying leaves. If we were to unite those branches . . . *(she hugs him)* the tree would no longer be divided, and all would return to its natural state: title, family, and possessions.

WILLIAM: *(Pulling away from her)* I don't dare think what you're suggesting.

DOWAGER: Don't be shy. Kiss my hand, take it between yours, and thus we shall surmount whatever differences might divide our noble family.

WILLIAM: But . . . God forgive me . . . you're proposing . . . our betrothal?

DOWAGER: Only for the good of the House of Derby.

WILLIAM: When my brother's body has scarcely been placed in the tomb?

DOWAGER: I am sure my noble husband would have no objections.

WILLIAM: How could he object when he's dead?

DOWAGER: Even if he were alive. And if he did, I would persuade him to come to reason.

WILLIAM: Say it clearly now. You want to be the Countess of Derby again.

DOWAGER: I still am.

WILLIAM: Only as a dowager. But then someday your daughters would inherit the whole estate.

DOWAGER: Can you think of anyone with greater claim?

WILLIAM: By heaven and earth! His death has scarcely occurred before the salt of your tears is washed from your eyes! Even an animal, incapable of reason, would suffer a more enduring sorrow.

DOWAGER: *(With dignity)* My sorrow is more intense than that of even the most sentimental animal.

WILLIAM: Never—hear me well, my lady—never will I sully my brother's bed with incestuous nuptials that God himself would disavow.

DOWAGER: Leave God out of this. We're talking about family matters and, with all due respect, as far as I know, God isn't a Derby.

WILLIAM: Let us put an end to this unpleasant conversation.

DOWAGER: As you wish. But if you have so little concern for the peace and harmony of our family, you'll have to face the consequences.

WILLIAM: And you, madam, judicial review. I shall go forthwith to Her Majesty's magistrates. It will be the most scandalous lawsuit in memory, but I will not marry you, nor shall you usurp what rightly belongs to the Sixth Earl of Derby.

DOWAGER: And I shall go forthwith to my lawyers to defend my husband's last will and testament. I am a bad enemy.

WILLIAM: I don't doubt that.

DOWAGER: What would your noble brother say about your attitude, which offends not only the honor of the House of Derby but also the virtue of his beloved wife.

WILLIAM: *(Declaring the meeting over)* Your humble servant, madam.

DOWAGER: And I, sir, ever your dutiful sister-in-law. *(She starts to exit but then turns and asks in her sweetest voice)* By the way, did you poison your brother?

WILLIAM: Your question is an affront.

DOWAGER: I only repeat what everyone's saying, not only in drawing rooms but on the streets and in the taverns.

WILLIAM: That's slander.

DOWAGER: You'll have to prove it to stop the talk.

WILLIAM: How?

DOWAGER: By taking vengeance on the murderers, cleansing with their blood the honor of our name.

WILLIAM: But no one knows who did it or even if he was murdered.

DOWAGER: They say it was the Catholics.

WILLIAM: There are Catholics all over Europe. I couldn't wipe them all out if I lived a thousand years.

DOWAGER: If you can't get them all, at least kill a few dozen.

WILLIAM: You want me beheaded in the Tower of London?

DOWAGER: Better honor without a head than a head without honor.

WILLIAM: I regret not being able to satisfy you, but I need mine for other duties.

DOWAGER: No doubt to bury it in the sand, like an ostrich.

WILLIAM: *(Saying goodbye)* My lady . . .

DOWAGER: My lord ... *(Just before exiting)* Oh, one last thing. To prove to you my noble feelings, when the period of mourning is over and I hold the first banquet at my palace, I shall reserve for you the place of honor at my table. At my side.

WILLIAM: It will be a privilege to dine next to the most charming lady in all England.

DOWAGER: And for me, to have at my right side my lord Earl of Derby.

(Exit the Dowager Countess)

WILLIAM: I wouldn't sit next to her if I were drunk! That bitch would be capable of poisoning my food. I'm sure she's the one who started the rumor that I'm responsible for my brother's death. I admit that I've run a sword through nobles and even kings ... but only in the tragedies I write. The slut! First she convinces my brother to disinherit me, and now she wants to marry me to get her hands on my fortune, too. But she's right about one thing. My only way out of these sad straits is to marry a rich heiress. Young, virtuous, and, if possible, attractive. Now where will I find such a rare bird as that?

(Enter Mary)

MARY: My beloved little dove, you seem so worried. Is there something I can do to help?

WILLIAM: I'm afraid not.

MARY: Would you like me to get undressed?

WILLIAM: Do you think all difficulties can be resolved through the pleasures of the flesh?

MARY: *(Disappointed)* Do you no longer think me pretty?

WILLIAM: You're delectable, but when I think that I must marry some insipid maiden whom I don't even know, I have no more appetite for lovemaking than a newborn babe.

MARY: You're going to take a wife?

WILLIAM: I have no choice.

MARY: And what will become of me when you're married?

WILLIAM: You'll serve your mistress and obey her wishes.

MARY: You would deprive me of the pleasure of offering you my affection?

WILLIAM: No one can make me renounce the most delicate flower of my gardens.

MARY: *(Happily)* Oh, thank you, my lord. I love you. *(She kisses him.)* And who is the fortunate lady?

WILLIAM: I don't know. I spend so many hours shut away here with my books and my writing, never going to balls or receptions, that I scarcely know any noble young maidens. Tell me, Mary, whom would you choose for my wife?

MARY: I'm not the right person to advise you.

WILLIAM: Servants know the masters they serve better than anyone. What do they say about the Baroness of Richmond?

MARY: That she's cross-eyed. And cross-eyed women have bad tempers.

WILLIAM: And what do you think about the niece of the Duke of York?

MARY: Too old. She must be at least twenty-eight.

WILLIAM: And Lady Blint?

MARY: I wouldn't recommend her. They tell a lot of stories about her.

WILLIAM: Well, I can't think of anyone else.

MARY: They say the Earl of Oxford's daughter is discreet and virtuous.

WILLIAM: But she's become accustomed to expensive whims. I'd have to give magnificent parties that would cost me a fortune.

MARY: Her father is one of the richest gentlemen in all England.

WILLIAM: That's true. I shall have to go to the castle at Oxfordshire to meet his daughter. By the way, I hope you've never told anyone about my writing.

MARY: Oh, no, milord. I'd sooner cut out my tongue.

WILLIAM: I don't even want to think what someone as proud and haughty as the Earl of Oxford would say about me if he found out. But I must settle these affairs at once. Send Costrand to me.

MARY: May I ask for a kiss?

WILLIAM: No. Go away. But you can take one without asking.
 (He kisses her. Exit Mary)

WILLIAM: *(To his listeners)* Sometimes she gets a bit annoying with her displays of affection. Ah, but when I have to get along without her, how I shall miss her.
 (Enter Costrand)

COSTRAND: Milord.

WILLIAM: I have to speak to you.

COSTRAND: What have I done wrong this time?

WILLIAM: Nothing that I know of. But you must never reveal to anyone what I am about to tell you. It is a matter of the utmost secrecy.

COSTRAND: You frighten me, sir.

WILLIAM: You know how I spend most of my time, for you are the one who fashions my pens and brings me paper.

COSTRAND: Yes, milord.

WILLIAM: Have you never asked yourself what it is that I write with them?

COSTRAND: Those are matters of the noble Earl that do not concern me.

WILLIAM: Well, I shall reveal it to you. I write poems, sonnets . . .

COSTRAND: Sonwhats?

WILLIAM: But, above all, plays—plays that someday will be performed by actors.

COSTRAND: Actors, they say, are the devil's messengers who incite people to vice and wicked ways.

WILLIAM: That's the reputation attributed to them. Although there must indeed be something shameful about the theater when a nobleman cannot put his name and coat of arms to a work for the stage without discrediting himself. Do you understand what I'm saying?

COSTRAND: Not very well, sir.

WILLIAM: That's why I'm obliged to hide my identity and have someone else appear as the author. So I've decided that you should sign the works with your name.

COSTRAND: Me, sir? Costrand?

WILLIAM: Costrand.

COSTRAND: You mean to say that you would write and I . . . ? With all due respect, milord, I don't believe it's a good idea.

WILLIAM: You're going to disobey my orders?

COSTRAND: God preserve me from that, my lord. But there is a serious drawback. I don't know how to sign my name.

WILLIAM: Your ignorance goes that far?

COSTRAND: I can neither read nor write. I've been so busy serving your lordship from morning to night that I haven't had time for such petty things.

WILLIAM: Not even if I guide your hand?

COSTRAND: I'm very clumsy when it comes to such fine skills. Perhaps my mother. She's a seamstress and does delicate needlework.

WILLIAM: What an idea! A woman! Why, that would bring even greater shame than my own signature.

COSTRAND: Then you ought to seek another person.

WILLIAM: Who?

COSTRAND: I don't know anyone who can write. Although maybe . . .

WILLIAM: Yes? Speak up.

COSTRAND: In the company of actors who are performing in the square there is one from my mother's town with whom I've struck up a friendship.

WILLIAM: What town is that?

COSTRAND: Stratford, sir. Stratford-on-Avon.

WILLIAM: And he'd know how to write his name?

COSTRAND: I believe so. He seems like a clever young man. Although, like everyone in his trade, he's a bit of a libertine. He's a rogue who's chased after all the maids of the region. And even some of the lads, or so say the gossips. But ask Mary. She knows him well.

WILLIAM: *(Apprehensively)* Mary?

COSTRAND: The rascal has such a way of talking, so free and easy, that he dazzles all the lasses with his tomfoolery.

WILLIAM: What is this scallawag's name?

COSTRAND: I've already told you how insolent he is. He has the nerve to call himself William, just like the noble Earl.

WILLIAM: Bring him to me.

COSTRAND: Right away, my lord. *(He exits.)*

WILLIAM: Mary! Mary!

MARY: *(Entering)* Milord.

WILLIAM: What have you been up to with that actor named William?

MARY: Nothing, milord. He's such a bold one that I avoid his company.

WILLIAM: That's not what I've heard.

MARY: Whoever says anything else is lying. It must have been Costrand. Costrand's got a grudge against him. They even got into a fight over a crude compliment he paid me.

WILLIAM: Good for Costrand.

MARY: Although after that they drank a few tankards of ale and had the audacity to bet twopence on which one would kiss me first.

WILLIAM: The good-for-nothing swine!

MARY: *(Coquettishly)* Would you have been dismayed if one of them had won the twopence?

WILLIAM: Of course. I am your master, and I must keep guard over your virtue until the day a man of your own station takes you to the altar.

MARY: Is your lordship jealous?

WILLIAM: I am as I please. Get undressed!

MARY: With pleasure. I assure you that you won't be sorry.
(William has unfastened his doublet, and Mary is quickly taking off her clothes when there is a knock at the door.)

WILLIAM: Go see who it is. And cover yourself up!
(Mary puts her clothes back on and opens one of the bookcases, which she then closes at once.)

MARY: It's William, milord!

WILLIAM: Have him come in.

MARY: Don't believe anything he tells you. If he says I gratified him in any way, it's a lie. A lie! I swear on my mother's good health.

WILLIAM: Your mother is dead, you hussy!
(Mary leads in Shakespeare, who cannot take his eyes off her.)

SHAKESPEARE: What an enchanting vision! The sun of your beauty lights up the darkness of this chamber.

MARY: His lordship awaits you.

SHAKESPEARE: Thank you for lighting the fire of my heart so early in the morning.

MARY: Your heart is that sensitive?

SHAKESPEARE: You should know.

WILLIAM: Enough of your palaver and get over here, hooligan!

SHAKESPEARE: Are you speaking to me, sir?

WILLIAM: I don't see anyone else here.

SHAKESPEARE: Then you must be confused, my lord. I'm not Hooligan. I'm William.

WILLIAM: Both are true statements. And you, Mary, stand outside the door and see that no one can hear our conversation.
(Exit Mary)

SHAKESPEARE: So grave is the matter you wish to tell me?

WILLIAM: Don't speak until you're told to.

SHAKESPEARE: May I sit down?

WILLIAM: As you please, but be quiet and listen.

SHAKESPEARE: I'm all ears, milord.

WILLIAM: They tell me you know how to read and write.

SHAKESPEARE: *(After a pause)* Am I to speak?

WILLIAM: I'm asking you a question.

SHAKESPEARE: Forgive me, sir, but I cannot tell when you want me to be quiet and when you want me to speak.

WILLIAM: Are you making fun of me?

SHAKESPEARE: God forbid, but the question is a mite pointless. I'm an actor. I have to be able to read the roles that are given to me. Back in my hometown I learned to read at school, the only one I've attended.

WILLIAM: Just answer yes or no.

SHAKESPEARE: Yes. *(He raises a finger.)* May I ask for a clarification?

WILLIAM: You may.

SHAKESPEARE: What do you want from me?

WILLIAM: To offer you the opportunity to earn some money.

SHAKESPEARE: How much?

WILLIAM: Let's say a pound. And later another pound. And then another.

SHAKESPEARE: For a pound I'd do almost anything. Except kill a man.

WILLIAM: That's not at issue. Just your signature on the title page of some plays.

SHAKESPEARE: Not just my signature but my own portrait. I'm quite able to write them myself from start to finish. I've done so several times, but the director of my company is an ignoramus, and he's thrown the pages in my face.

WILLIAM: Your signature will suffice. But first I need to know something about your life to be sure your name has not been besmirched by some dishonor.

SHAKESPEARE: My family is honorable. My father is a town alderman, and my wife belongs to a family of landowners.

WILLIAM: Then why have you chosen such a profession?

SHAKESPEARE: It's a long story.

WILLIAM: I'm listening.

SHAKESPEARE: I was born in a little town on the Avon River. I was apprenticed to a glover, my family's trade. And I assure you that we made the finest gloves of the softest leathers. There were long ones, short ones with cuffs, ones with lace trim . . .

WILLIAM: Enough of gloves! Why did you leave your trade?

SHAKESPEARE: An unfortunate episode obliged me to flee the town with the game wardens right on my tail. Are you an avid hunter?

WILLIAM: Like all noblemen.

SHAKESPEARE: Then you will understand me.

WILLIAM: You were caught poaching?

SHAKESPEARE: A deer, milord. I was strolling one afternoon in the forests of Sir Thomas Lucy, a wealthy man whose power is equaled by his bad temper, when suddenly the deer appeared. It was large, well formed, with magnificent antlers, and it danced before me like a wicked wench. I am not made of stone, and I became more and more excited as the cunning beast circled about me, daring me with his glance. The rogue even did his business in front of me as if to show me his scorn. Thus it was that impulsively I lifted my bow to my chest, shot off two arrows, and wounded him. I was about to finish him off with my dagger when the game warden appeared, the very one who had vowed to get even with me ever since the day he found me lying with his daughter. He shouted so wildly that the birds flew away in fear and the hares took refuge in their warrens.

WILLIAM: Poaching is punished with the severest of penalties.

SHAKESPEARE: It was Heaven's will that my legs were swifter than his.

WILLIAM: Have you been in jail?

SHAKESPEARE: I came close because of some drinking bout or other youthful follies . . . but I only know prison bars from the outside.

WILLIAM: Go on.

SHAKESPEARE: I ended up in London, where I tried my hand at several trades. As apprentice to a butcher and a coppersmith and in the print shop of some Frenchmen. But when I was a child I saw some actors in my town, and ever since my ambition has been to work in the theater. Finally, I was able to. I began by holding horses at the stage door. Then I became a servant to the actors until at last they let me play a minor role.

WILLIAM: You're a rogue, but you seem clever enough. What is your surname?

SHAKESPEARE: Shakpso or Shaksper. On every document they write it differently. The scribes in my region aren't known for the accuracy of their spelling.

WILLIAM: Shakp? There's no way to pronounce that without choking on it. Let's see. Write it out for me.

(Shakespeare does so, with his left hand.)

WILLIAM: You have dreadful handwriting. That's almost illegible.

SHAKESPEARE: That's because I'm left-handed.

WILLIAM: *(Picking up the paper)* If we added an "e" and joined the two words, we'd get Shakespeare. William Shakespeare. It's a difficult name that no one will remember. Although that doesn't matter. That's the way you'll sign my works.

SHAKESPEARE: But that would be a deception, an imposture no decent man can accept. At least not for a pound. Make it a pound and ten shillings.

WILLIAM: A pound and ten shillings for a simple signature! A guinea, that's as far as I'll go.

SHAKESPEARE: A pound and fivepence.

WILLIAM: Two.

SHAKESPEARE: Four.

WILLIAM: Three and ha'pence.

SHAKESPEARE: Done.

(Short pause while William takes out a couple of manuscripts from a cupboard.)

WILLIAM: Here are two manuscripts. Take them to the director of your theater.

SHAKESPEARE: He'll throw them in my face as he did with mine. He has a nasty disposition.

WILLIAM: He won't do that once he's read them.

SHAKESPEARE: And if he doesn't want to read them?

WILLIAM: Kidnap him if necessary, and hold him prisoner until he's finished reading.

SHAKESPEARE: He'd throw me out of the company, and I'd lose my job.

WILLIAM: On the contrary. He'll respect you more than ever.

SHAKESPEARE: It all seems very easy to you. I don't know, I don't know . . . *(glancing at the manuscripts)* Love's Labor's Lost? Since when is love labor?

WILLIAM: That doesn't concern you.

SHAKESPEARE: *The Jew of Malta* or *The Tragical History of Doctor Faustus,* now those are attractive titles. You could learn a lot from a master like Marlowe. *(He reads another title.)* The Two Gentlemen of Verona. In what part of England is that?

WILLIAM: In Italy.

SHAKESPEARE: Who cares what happens in that country? You ought to change these titles, believe me, sir. I'm in the business, and you're just an amateur.

WILLIAM: I've had enough of your insolence.

SHAKESPEARE: I say that for both our sakes.

WILLIAM: Enough!

SHAKESPEARE: And doesn't it occur to you that if I sign these plays I could usurp an honor that belongs solely to you?

WILLIAM: The House of Derby is related to the royal families of Scotland and England. That is my honor! No troupe of actors can bring honor to me. All they can do is let others know the beauty of my works.

SHAKESPEARE: But they'll say I am a bird who adorns himself in someone else's feathers.

WILLIAM: What difference can that make to you? Be gone.

SHAKESPEARE: Aren't you forgetting something, your lordship?
(He makes a gesture indicating money.)

WILLIAM: *(Giving him some coins)* A pound and threepence.

SHAKESPEARE: And ha'pence. For each manuscript.

WILLIAM: You know your arithmetic?

SHAKESPEARE: Well enough to multiply by two.

WILLIAM: *(Giving him the rest of the money)* Schercep or Shekip or Shakespeare or whatever your name is, I detest shameless, mercenary rogues like you. I don't like you. Not one bit.

SHAKESPEARE: With all the respect due your dignified rank, I don't like you either. And I fear I also won't like your writing.

WILLIAM: Out!

SHAKESPEARE: Your obedient servant, milord. I shall take my leave, without delay.
(He exits hastily.)

WILLIAM: What an irritating lout. He's an ignorant, uneducated womanizer and, from what they tell me, a poor actor to boot. And a miser! How he delighted in counting the coins. So why did I pick him instead of someone more cultured and learned? So that no one would ever believe such a fellow could be the author of my plays. How could that scallawag know the language and feelings of kings and noblemen when the only chambers he has entered are stables and kitchens? And how could he place the action in so many countries when he has never been away from the low-class neighborhoods of London? What could he know of law, medicine, alchemy, and music? And of history? And if all that weren't enough, he takes more than a pound from me for every work! That is what grieves me most, for the lawsuit my sister-in-law wages against me shows every sign of never ending, and the lawyers keep asking me for money. Let's hope that when I marry, the Oxford fortune will solve my financial problems.

(Enter Costrand and Mary with a basket of medals and insignia)

COSTRAND: Your lordship, it's time.

WILLIAM: Time for what?

MARY: Time to put on the finery and medals appropriate to your rank. For the wedding.

WILLIAM: Ah yes, the wedding. Already?

MARY: Already, milord. The Earl of Oxford, his family and followers are entering the chapel.

(Costrand and Mary begin to arrange William's medals and sashes.)

WILLIAM: And the actors? Are they ready?

COSTRAND: Everything is ready for the performance of the play you have written for this occasion.

WILLIAM: *(Ironically)* It is not I who wrote this comedy, but your friend William. Don't forget.

COSTRAND: *(Smiling, in complicity)* As you like it, milord.

WILLIAM: The plot revolves around fairies, elves, and magic spells. The queen of the fairies falls in love with an ass. *(Laughing at his own cleverness)* A little ass with a snout and enormous ears. *(Laughing again)* It's sublime!

COSTRAND: *(Putting in place the last medal)* The Order of the Garter! The highest honor the Queen bestows.

WILLIAM: How do I look?

COSTRAND: Oh, sir, when the bride sees your proud figure, she will outdo herself in compliments.

WILLIAM: I doubt it. She's so quiet and serious.

COSTRAND: Her seamstresses are putting the final touches on her garments so she may dazzle your guests.

WILLIAM: Frankly, Costrand, what do you think of my bride?

COSTRAND: Everyone praises her discretion.

WILLIAM: Of course she's discreet. She never says two words in a row. I confess that I'm frightened.

COSTRAND: The Earls of Derby have proven their valor in a thousand battles!

WILLIAM: War is less dangerous than marriage. And, to be sure, it doesn't last as long. But do you think her pretty?

COSTRAND: I would never presume . . .

WILLIAM: Do it this time.

COSTRAND: I do not dare . . .

WILLIAM: I command it.

COSTRAND: Well, in the dark, with the curtains drawn . . . beauty means very little during a romp in the bed. Tonight more than one man would wish himself in your place.

WILLIAM: I will not tolerate such shameful indecency!

COSTRAND: You insisted that I give you my opinion.

WILLIAM: It is a terrible sin to covet thy neighbor's wife, particularly if the neighbor is an earl.

MARY: They are waiting for your lordship. The archbishop is already at the altar.

WILLIAM: Oh, Mary, my dear Mary, you are the most precious gift God has granted me, even if I do not always express my gratitude as you deserve.

MARY: Don't say that, sir. May I kiss you? *(Kissing him)* When I think that this could be the last time.

WILLIAM: I already told you that the wedding changes nothing. No one is going to deprive me of your delightful company. *(To Costrand)* And you, what are you waiting for?

COSTRAND:Your orders, milord, so the musicians may begin the wedding march. *(Costrand turns on the tape recorder. Music.)* The ceremony has begun, sir.

WILLIAM: Couldn't we wait a little longer?

COSTRAND: I'm afraid not, sir.

WILLIAM: I feel weak.

MARY: *(She takes him by the hand)* Courage, milord. Let's go.

COSTRAND: *(Taking the other hand)* Let's go, my lord.

> *(Mary and Costrand between them, almost dragging him, take William to the door formed by one of the bookcases. A bright light from the other side suggests the church. All exit. After a pause, William reappears and turns off the tape recorder.)*

WILLIAM: *(He sits down, exhausted.)* What a day! I'm exhausted. First the church. With so many people, it was unbearably hot. And since the archbishop stammers a bit, I thought he'd never finish his sermon. Then the banquet. How they gobbled it up. As if they hadn't eaten in a year! And then the wine. The fortune it must all have cost me. Well, let's hope they still have enough spirit left to enjoy the staging of my play.

COSTRAND: *(Entering)* Milord, they all await your lordship and his lady to open the wedding ball.

WILLIAM: I can't right now. I'm soaking wet with sweat, and my feet are swollen.

COSTRAND: At the top of your coat of arms is the tireless eagle.

WILLIAM: They don't oblige eagles to dance!

> *(Costrand starts the tape recorder. Dance music of the period. William gets up and goes to the bookcase door to receive Lady Derby, who enters, wearing her wedding dress. William kisses her hand, and they begin to dance. Applause. Costrand remains onstage.)*

WILLIAM: My dear wife, you are as graceful as a gazelle, and you dance like an angel.

LADY DERBY: Did you say something?

WILLIAM: I said you dance like an angel.

LADY DERBY: *(Dully)* You are too kind.

> *(Pause. They continue dancing.)*

WILLIAM: I feel great joy because of our happy union.

LADY DERBY: What did you say?

WILLIAM: That I feel great joy.

LADY DERBY: You are too kind, my husband.

WILLIAM: And you, gentle lady? Do you not feel joy?

LADY DERBY: I appreciate my lord's kindness.

> *(The music and dancing end. Assisted by Costrand, William and Lady Derby sit down on chairs, side by side as if on a throne. Exit Costrand)*

WILLIAM: The servants of this household have paid you the homage you deserve.

LADY DERBY: In the house of my father, the Earl of Oxford, the servants are more numerous and better attired.

WILLIAM: They've shown you the stables.

LADY DERBY: Your horses don't seem very dashing. I shall ride the Spanish sorrel my father gave me.

WILLIAM: How do you like the castle?

LADY DERBY: It seems more of a fortress than a palace. When are you going to hang tapestries?

WILLIAM: They're already in place, my lady.

LADY DERBY: They barely cover the walls; they're threadbare.

WILLIAM: Your noble father, so famed for his affluence and magnanimity, will doubtless correct through his generosity the deficiencies that dismay you.

LADY DERBY: Indeed, my father is lavishly rich, but he is very annoyed by the meager allowance you have set aside for my personal expenses.

WILLIAM: A thousand pounds is a sizable sum, my lady.

LADY DERBY: That's what I used to spend on one ball gown.

WILLIAM: I trust your noble father will round out the sum so you may be fully satisfied.

LADY DERBY: You can forget my father's money. He has sworn not to let loose a single penny from his purse.

WILLIAM: I can't believe it.

LADY DERBY: He has also cut you off without a penny in his will.

WILLIAM: But why?

LADY DERBY: For your own good. To save you from the temptation of poisoning him as it is rumored you did with your brother.

WILLIAM: *(Indignantly)* That's a lie. A falsehood invented by that evil witch of a sister-in-law and her serpent's tongue.

LADY DERBY: Don't upset yourself. It's no dishonor. Such episodes are common in noble families when there's inheritance involved.

WILLIAM: I shall talk to your father.

LADY DERBY: Don't waste your time. My father would never fail to keep a pledge.

WILLIAM: Not a penny?

LADY DERBY: Not a penny. I trust that as a nobleman you will respect my father's honor.

WILLIAM: *(Undone)* Whatever you say.

LADY DERBY: You are too kind, my husband.
    (Sound of trumpets)

WILLIAM: My gracious lady, to conclude the happy celebration of our nuptials I have reserved a special surprise that I hope will please you.

LADY DERBY: A present?

WILLIAM: Something like that.

LADY DERBY: *(Brightening a bit)* A diamond tiara? A ruby bracelet?

WILLIAM: Much better than that. A fantastic comedy written in your honor.

LADY DERBY: I detest the theater. It bores me.

WILLIAM: This play will please you. It has elves, fairies, magic, and other amusing creations.

LADY DERBY: Fairies and elves have always seemed sheer stupidity to me.

WILLIAM: I am sure your sensitive and refined spirit will make you change your mind.

LADY DERBY: I doubt it.

DOWAGER: *(Entering)* I have come to pay my respects to the happy partners in wedlock.

WILLIAM: The countess and I appreciate your kindness.

DOWAGER: How pretty you are, my dear countess. And to think that envious minds said you're ugly and unattractive! Your seamstresses have performed miracles tonight so you are as radiant as the sun.

WILLIAM: Aren't you going to respond to your sister-in-law's compliments?

LADY DERBY: You are too kind, my lady.

DOWAGER: It matters not that your husband is twice your age or that you have no experience in handling the accounts of a county. Your joy will be as great as the generosity of my heart, which congratulates you on your happiness.

WILLIAM: Again, we offer you our thanks.

DOWAGER: My lord, allow me to kiss the bride. *(She does so with a certain irony.)* From now on, you will be the sister I never had.

LADY DERBY: You are too kind, my dear sister-in-law.

DOWAGER: What a cheerful, clever, nice person you are. You have all the qualities needed to make our long family gatherings pleasant occasions.

COSTRAND: *(Entering)* Milord, everything is ready for the performance.

WILLIAM: Then let it begin.

(Costrand turns on the tape recorder, and music is heard. Costrand exits. Shakespeare enters, costumed as a woman.)

SHAKESPEARE: Noble ladies and gentlemen. We are about to present a comedy, composed on the occasion of the solemn nuptials of the noble Earl and Countess of Derby. We humbly beg your pardon for any faults you may find in the performance.

LADY DERBY: What a dreadful woman!

WILLIAM: Do you perchance not know that only men are allowed to act in the theater?

DOWAGER: What poor taste, having a play at a wedding feast.

SHAKESPEARE: The title of this work is *A Midsummer Night's Dream*.
(William applauds. Lady Derby closes her eyes.)

WILLIAM: Applaud, my love.
(Two actors appear: Mary, dressed as a man, and Costrand, dressed as a woman.)

SHAKESPEARE: *(Reciting)* ". . . our nuptial hour
Draws on apace . . .
(Mary and Costrand join in.)
four happy days bring in
Another moon. But oh, methinks, how slow
This old moon wanes!"
(Lady Derby is asleep.)

WILLIAM: For goodness sake, my lady, don't fall asleep.

SHAKESPEARE: "Four days will quickly steep themselves in night.
(Mary and Costrand join in.)
Four nights will quickly dream away the time,
And then the moon, like to a silver bow
New-bent in heaven, shall behold the night
Of our solemnities."

LADY DERBY: What idiot is responsible for that mumbo jumbo?

WILLIAM: But madam . . .

LADY DERBY: *(Preparing to go back to sleep)* As for me . . .

WILLIAM: Just because the play deals with a midsummer night's dream doesn't mean you have to sleep. Open your eyes!

SHAKESPEARE: "Go, Philostrate,

Stir up the Athenian youth to merriments.

Awake the pert and nimble spirit of mirth."

(The other two actors begin to dance.)

WILLIAM: *(Exasperated, to Lady Derby)* Don't go to sleep, dammit!

LADY DERBY: *(Frightened)* But my lord!

WILLIAM: Wake up or I'll choke you!

DOWAGER: Is something wrong with the bride?

WILLIAM: Nothing that concerns you! *(To the Dowager Countess)* You be quiet! *(To Lady Derby)* And you, open your eyes! *(To Shakespeare, who is also frightened and has stopped reciting his speech)* And you? Why have you stopped? Go on!

SHAKESPEARE: "Turn melancholy forth to funerals,

The pale companion is not for our pomp.

But I will wed thee in another key,

With pomp, with triumph, and with reveling."

(The three actors—Shakespeare, Mary, and Costrand—begin a lively dance. While William watches in fascination, Lady Derby begins to snore, softly but clearly.)

CURTAIN

Act II

(William is onstage. Enter Mary.)

MARY: Your lordship! Your lordship! Someone has just arrived from London who asks to be received most urgently.

WILLIAM: Can't you see I'm busy?

MARY: Forgive my boldness, sir, but he insists that the matter is serious.

WILLIAM: Who is it?

MARY: William, my lord. That actor friend of Costrand's.

WILLIAM: And you say he's just arrived?

MARY: A few moments ago.

WILLIAM: You're lying! I saw you last night from the tower window. You and that impertinent lout heading to the garden.

MARY: How could you see when there was no moon? I took him out to the stable so he could sleep in the hayloft. He arrived so late that I asked him to await the new day in order not to disturb your lordship's rest.

WILLIAM: You spent the night with him?

MARY: You know full well that my body and my love belong only to you.

WILLIAM: Then why did you not come to my bedchamber?

MARY: It was Tuesday. And you have set aside Tuesday to be dutiful to your wife.

WILLIAM: I don't know. I find you rather agitated.

MARY: It must be my impatience for your kisses, my beloved little rabbit, my little dove . . .

WILLIAM: Enough of domestic animals. Have him come in.

MARY: Would you like me to get undressed?

WILLIAM: No! Now be gone.

(Mary lets Shakespeare in and then exits.)

SHAKESPEARE: Your lordship.

WILLIAM: What news do you bring from London?

SHAKESPEARE: Very alarming news, sir. I am in danger. That is why I have dared to present myself here.

WILLIAM: What has happened?

SHAKESPEARE: A terrible thing. An insurrection. A conspiracy against Her Majesty. The Earl of Essex and other noblemen tried to dethrone Queen Elizabeth and give the crown to King James of Scotland.

WILLIAM: And what do you have to do with those noblemen?

SHAKESPEARE: Nothing, milord, but it all began in our theater.

WILLIAM: A conspiracy in a theater?

SHAKESPEARE: You have to save me, sir. Have pity on me, seeing as how it was your lordship who put me at risk.

WILLIAM: I?

SHAKESPEARE: I fear for my life.

WILLIAM: Calm down and tell me all about it.

SHAKESPEARE: Very well. First may I have a sip of water? *(He drinks)* Several days ago a messenger from the Earl of Essex came to the theater for the purpose of having us stage *The Tragedy of King Richard the Second.* You remember the work, milord?

WILLIAM: Why wouldn't I, considering that I wrote it?

SHAKESPEARE: You realize the malice behind such a proposal? *Richard II,* no less.

WILLIAM: It's a beautiful drama.

SHAKESPEARE: But it tells how one king is deposed and supplanted by another, how for the good of the people it is legitimate to dethrone a king, or a queen. You see their intention?

WILLIAM: Vaguely.

SHAKESPEARE: Phyllips, our director, suspected something shady in it and made excuses, saying the play would not attract enough of an audience. But the messenger insisted. He persisted so much that Phyllips ending up agreeing, although for just one performance. He should never have done so! Because as we were reciting the last lines of the last act there arose amid the audience a terrible uproar such as had never before been seen at the Globe Theater. May I have another sip of water?

WILLIAM: No! Go on.

SHAKESPEARE: My mouth feels so dry, just as it did on that ill-fated evening. The scandal that broke out, the shouts and insults against the Queen, made us stop the performance. My legs still tremble when I think about it.

WILLIAM: Are you going to finish the story?

SHAKESPEARE: Then they all went out into the street, with their swords drawn, shouting, "Long live King James." And they headed to the royal palace. But the good people of London, as frightened as we, hid in their houses and did not join the rebellion.

WILLIAM: And Her Majesty, the Queen?

SHAKESPEARE: They say that she was beside herself, exclaiming that she was Richard II and that she would make an example of the Earl of Essex and all his followers. Thus they were overwhelmed and imprisoned in the Tower of London to be brought to justice.

WILLIAM: The noble Earl of Essex rebelling against the Queen!

SHAKESPEARE: Behind all this there must be some intrigue of love or disdain, both of which are poor counselors. The Earl was Her Majesty's favorite. He received her royal favor—and perhaps more intimate favors as well.

WILLIAM: You dare to judge the Queen's conduct?

SHAKESPEARE: They say that the Queen became furious when she learned Essex had a lover. And that she angrily threw him out of her bedchamber. And they also say that Essex, who doesn't hold his tongue, responded to the Queen that she had become old and unbearable and that her soul was even more twisted than her spine.

WILLIAM: That's enough gossip.

SHAKESPEARE: Enough said.

(Pause)

WILLIAM: What I can't imagine is what you want from me.

SHAKESPEARE: They have jailed Phyllips for allowing the rebels to take charge of the theater, and if I am not mistaken, they are getting the noose ready to hang him. And my name appears as the author of the fateful work. I don't want to end up like him, milord! I'm young. I have a wife and children. Nothing would please me less than swinging in a prison courtyard with my tongue hanging out.

WILLIAM: Besides being a coward, you're presumptuous. *(Laughing)* Don't worry. No one will attribute to you the least responsibility. The whole court well knows you did not write that work. And they would not dare to accuse someone of my noble rank. Why, they all laugh when they see your name on the quartos sold by the book dealers.

SHAKESPEARE: Ridicule was not part of our bargain, sir. But I swear to the devil that if it's going to save me from the scaffold, I welcome it. Between the noose and laughter, I gladly choose laughter.

(He starts to laugh boisterously.)

WILLIAM: Stop that annoying laughter.

SHAKESPEARE: *(Stopping his laughter abruptly)* As you command, milord.

(He remains standing where he is.)

WILLIAM: What are you waiting for?

SHAKESPEARE: There is another, rather delicate matter we need to deal with, your lordship.

WILLIAM: I want no more dealings with you.

SHAKESPEARE: Wait until you find out what it is. *(Taking a handkerchief out of his pocket)* Have you not sometimes seen a handkerchief like this, with your coat of arms embroidered on it?

WILLIAM: Where'd you get that?

SHAKESPEARE: It was given to me by a servant of the Earl of Essex—in exchange for some crowns. The rumormonger is saying he found it in his master's bedchamber.

WILLIAM: What evil are you plotting?

SHAKESPEARE: Quite the contrary, sir. I imagined that your lordship would be pleased to have it back, to allay any suspicions about Lady Derby.

WILLIAM: Give me the handkerchief and go away.

SHAKESPEARE: As they say the Earl of Essex is a libertine, and people are so malicious, I thought it wise to ransom it, no matter what price the rogue asked.

WILLIAM: All right. Here are some crowns, and get out of my sight.

SHAKESPEARE: *(Counting them)* Only ten, milord? I paid twenty-five.

WILLIAM: Scoundrel!

SHAKESPEARE: The price seemed very high to me, too. But I thought the honor of a family so noble as that of your lordship was well worth it.

WILLIAM: *(Giving him the rest of the money)* Here it is. Now be gone.

SHAKESPEARE: Don't worry, milord. Sometimes appearances are deceiving. Unfortunately, the Earl of Essex, with his head cut off, will be in no state to clarify matters.

WILLIAM: Not a word more or I'll skewer you with my sword.

SHAKESPEARE: You needn't go through all that trouble for me. God be with you.

WILLIAM: And with you, all of hell's demons!

(Exit SHAKESPEARE*)*

By Heaven! My wife's handkerchief, in that cursed villain's bedchamber. May he go to hell. My wife deceives me, she has placed horns upon my brow. I am a cuckold! I never did like that wretched Essex. I kept my feelings hidden because he was the Queen's lover and Her Majesty was so infatuated by him. So he strutted about the court, more arrogant than a gamecock, shamelessly eyeing all the ladies as if they were so many hens in his chicken coop. But I never thought he'd pay attention to my lackluster lady. The slyboots! Here she pretends to be so modest that she allows me to share her bed only on Tuesdays, reluctantly at that. And she won't even take off her nightgown. And the strumpet gives herself to the Queen's official lover. If Her Majesty ever finds out, she'll have all our heads. To think that this handkerchief of Italian linen was the first present I offered her as a token of our betrothal. What obscene acts the filthy thing has witnessed! *(Throwing it on the table)* What I most regret is that the Queen has beaten me to it, and I'll not be able to kill the knave myself. But the other traitor remains to satisfy my vengeance. I'll wrap this very handkerchief about her neck until her eyes cloud over, her mouth ceases to breathe, and her sinful body falls lifeless at my feet. Oh! Oh!

LADY DERBY: *(Entering)* I thought I heard you scream. Does some ill beset you?

WILLIAM: I'm fine. I scream because I feel like it. I am in full command of my throat.

LADY DERBY: Of course you are, milord.

WILLIAM: *(With a sinister smile)* And also of yours. Let me see your throat, gentle lady.
(Unbuttoning her dress)

LADY DERBY: I beg you, respect my modesty.

WILLIAM: Only a stranger's hands can besmirch a lady's modesty ... *(Opening her dress wider)* not the hands of a husband to whom God has entrusted your virtue.

LADY DERBY: I fail to understand.

WILLIAM: Tonight I would hold a great celebration in our bed.

LADY DERBY: But it isn't Tuesday!

WILLIAM: *(With another sinister and threatening smile)* Under certain circumstances the day of the week matters not. Have them bring the finest sheets and the most intoxicating perfumes, let the musicians regale us with their sweetest melodies. And you, fair lady, clad yourself in your most revealing gown so we may relish the sight of your most appealing throat.

LADY DERBY: *(Alarmed)* You may rely always on my obedience.

WILLIAM: It shall be a night you'll never forget. Or, more to the point, that you'll forget immediately. *(He laughs.)* It is my wish that you adorn your pillow with that handkerchief I gave you when first we met.

LADY DERBY: *(Growing pale)* Why such a whim as that?

WILLIAM: It has my coat of arms, embroidered in gold and surrounded by little red strawberries. Go look for it.

LADY DERBY: I am so sorry, sir, but I fear the handkerchief has been misplaced.

WILLIAM: Then have the servants search every chest in your bedchamber until they find it.

LADY DERBY: They already looked, but it was not there.

WILLIAM: Did you perhaps misplace it in some other bedchamber when you were visiting the court?

LADY DERBY: You are insulting my virtue.

WILLIAM: Your virtue, madam, was lost with your handkerchief in the private chambers of an infamous and treacherous gentleman.

LADY DERBY: I will not tolerate such an insult!

WILLIAM: Do you dare to deny that you have been unfaithful to your wifely duties?

LADY DERBY: What are you saying?

WILLIAM: Here is the proof of my shame, and of yours. *(Taking the handkerchief, he holds it up to his eyes.)* The handkerchief! "Il fazzoletto," as the Italians would say. The snot rag, to put it in common language. The one that will never be discovered in your rooms because it was found in the adulterous chamber of the Earl of Essex, your lover.

LADY DERBY: That's a lie. I never set foot in his chamber.

WILLIAM: That's because he carried you over the threshold.

LADY DERBY: Perhaps I left it accidentally in some hall of the court.

WILLIAM: Your agitation betrays you.

LADY DERBY: Why should I not be agitated by such slander? The Earl of Essex himself will confirm the falsity of such an accusation.

WILLIAM: I assure you that the despicable Earl will retain a grave silence.

LADY DERBY: He is too noble for that.

WILLIAM: At this very moment his head is on a pike at the Tower of London.

LADY DERBY: What are you saying?

WILLIAM: Brought to justice as a traitor to the Crown.

LADY DERBY: *(Feeling faint)* It's not possible.

WILLIAM: *(Cruelly)* His lips, which enjoyed your kisses; his eyes, which delighted in your gaze; his ears, which heard your sighs are now food for the crows that hasten to the great feast.

LADY DERBY: I beg of you, don't continue.

WILLIAM: As for you, madam, I regret that I must deprive you of this evening's banquet, but my impatience does not allow me to wait so long. Have you prayed tonight? If you have any crime unreconciled as yet to Heaven and grace, solicit for it straight, for you are about to yield up your sinful soul.

LADY DERBY: Alas, my lord, what may you mean by that?

WILLIAM: This handkerchief, witness to your treason, shall be the instrument by which God punishes your infamy.
(He wraps the handkerchief about her neck.)

LADY DERBY: You're hurting me, my lord. Don't pull it so tight. I can't breathe!

WILLIAM: Die, beloved and deceitful wife!

LADY DERBY: *(In a blood-curdling scream)* Have mercy!

WILLIAM: Thus an Earl of Derby cleanses the honor of his house, on whose noble coat of arms there has never been a set of horns.

LADY DERBY: *(Freeing herself from the handkerchief)* Help! Guardsmen! Help!

WILLIAM: *(Chasing her)* You shall not escape my revenge. Adulteress! Traitor!

LADY DERBY: Help!
(Enter Costrand in alarm)

COSTRAND: My lady?

WILLIAM: What are you doing here?

COSTRAND: I thought I heard you calling me.

WILLIAM: No one asked for you. Get back to your work.

DOWAGER: *(Entering)* What are these dreadful screams? What is happening here?

WILLIAM: Nothing that concerns you.

DOWAGER: I was just coming to pay my respects, but I see I have arrived at a most inopportune moment.

LADY DERBY: Protect me, my lady. This monster has tried to strangle me.

DOWAGER: Your lord husband?

LADY DERBY: He, he . . . had a handkerchief.

WILLIAM: I have my motives.

DOWAGER: How horrible! Come to my arms, my child. I shall save you from the clutches of this monster.

WILLIAM: Ask the adulteress the reason for my anger.

LADY DERBY: Lies, nothing but lies.

DOWAGER: You, an adulteress? Has he gone mad?

LADY DERBY: It must come of writing so much.

DOWAGER: What does he write?

LADY DERBY: I know not. He shuts himself up in here like a ferret in a burrow.

WILLIAM: My writing has nothing to do with the affairs of this indecent bitch!

DOWAGER: No one is going to insult this innocent creature in my presence. *(To Costrand)* You shall be our bodyguard. In his state he's capable of all manner of atrocity. Call the palace guards so they may protect us.

LADY DERBY: Have the stable hands prepare my horses and my carriage for departure. Tell the maids to prepare my luggage.

COSTRAND: Yes, milady.

LADY DERBY: I shall go with my retinue to my father's castle.

DOWAGER: I shall accompany you. If he tries to strangle you, he'll have to strangle us both.

LADY DERBY: But before I leave, give me my handkerchief. I never liked it. Those little red strawberries seem to me ridiculous, lacking in good taste. But I want to keep it as evidence of insults I shall never forget.

DOWAGER: I, too, shall never forget this disgraceful scene. *(In an authoritarian tone)* Give her the handkerchief!

WILLIAM: *(Defeated, hands it over)* May Mary bring me a glass of the strongest wine from my cellars.

LADY DERBY: I should like to remind you that the little bitch is not your servant but mine, and she will leave with me. You'll have to find another strumpet for your bed.

DOWAGER: This is not the end of this grievous offense. You'll be hearing from us. Come, my dear. . . .

LADY DERBY: Ever your obedient wife, my good husband.

WILLIAM: Your humble servant, my good ladies.

(Lady Derby, the Dowager Countess, and Costrand exit)

The devil take that damned, pandering busybody! As for you, my good wife, my eternal gratitude. I shall no longer have to hear your complaints about how poor my house is, nor shall I have to hand over your monthly allowance of a thousand pounds nor endure every Tuesday the frigidity of a body that apparently heats up only for adulterous ardors. But what if she were innocent, and it were all just a trick invented by that scoundrel to get my twenty-five pounds? Ah, fate's cruel mockery! Such diabolic doubt. I shall compose a tragedy around this disturbing intrigue as a warning to all husbands.

(A judge enters, led in by Costrand, who is carrying a pile of documents. Costrand is dressed as a court clerk and will take notes throughout the scene.)

JUDGE: I am the Chief Judge of the Supreme Court. Her Majesty has designated me to pronounce sentence on the lawsuit milord has brought relative to your noble brother's legacy.

WILLIAM: It is about time we resolve that annoying suit!

JUDGE: New charges have been brought against your lordship, and you must respond to them.

WILLIAM: Against me? But who could accuse me of anything?

JUDGE: The Dowager Countess of Derby and your noble wife.

WILLIAM: My slut of a wife has conspired with that harpy of a sister-in-law to make up God knows what lies. It's certainly true that in this country justice is a mockery!

JUDGE: I insist that your lordship respect this court.

WILLIAM: And I insist that the court respect my noble lineage!

JUDGE: In the name of Her Majesty the Queen, this court will now come to order. *(To Costrand)* Call the Dowager Countess of Derby and Lady Derby. *(Enter the Dowager Countess and Lady Derby)*
Be seated, miladies, and express your grievances.

DOWAGER: The Countess and I have the painful duty of appearing before this court and accusing the Earl of Derby of grave crimes that affect the honor of our family and even the security of the Realm.

WILLIAM: What in God's name is the harpy talking about?

JUDGE: I beg your silence, milord. Milady, you may proceed.

DOWAGER: Many are the abuses perpetrated on my property by my good brother-in-law, and not only with respect to honoring the boundaries. He dares to use my possessions as if they were his own.

WILLIAM: In justice they ought to be mine.

DOWAGER: Your Honor should know that his servants have cut down a half hundred of my trees.

WILLIAM: They needed them to support the roofs of their houses.

DOWAGER: Oaks, noble oaks, Your Honor, under whose shade my late, lamented husband used to relax on spring afternoons.

WILLIAM: He can't do that now.

DOWAGER: They changed the course of my irrigation ditches to steal my water.

WILLIAM: Because our fields were dry.

DOWAGER: Thus they put my poor sheep at risk of dying from thirst. Has Your Honor ever heard the sorrowful bleat of thirsty lambs? It tears at your heart.

WILLIAM: My sheep, too, have the right to drink.

DOWAGER: And the Earl himself has committed the grave offense of poaching in my forests.

WILLIAM: I only hunted partridge! And I swear that I shot not a single one of those humble birds unless it was flying. You've stolen my land, my lady, but surely you don't lay claim as well to the skies of England.

DOWAGER: These misdeeds, and many others about which I shall remain silent in order not to weary Your Honor, are all punishable by law. But my kind and charitable nature prevents me from presenting further accusations. As long as these things don't happen again, of course. But there are other matters, infinitely more serious, that I feel impelled to denounce. These are matters that disturb my conscience during the day and prevent me from sleeping at night.

WILLIAM: No doubt my brother's ghost, horrified by your wickedness, is tugging at your feet.

DOWAGER: I beg that the good scribe record the insults that spew from his filthy mouth. And you, my lord, you should know that my husband and his ghost would lovingly kiss my feet.

JUDGE: You may proceed, madam.

DOWAGER: I refer to his writing, to which he dedicates all his time with an energy and passion so boundless as to be highly suspicious.

LADY DERBY: Secret writings.

DOWAGER: Whose content he reveals to no one and which he keeps hidden in his burrow like a ferret. Isn't that so, Countess?

LADY DERBY: Like a ferret!

WILLIAM: To write is perchance a crime?

DOWAGER: That depends upon what is being written. I, too, write: innocent letters to my cousin in Scotland and to my friends at Christmas. But I suggest that the Crown's censors examine the Earl's writings; they may well contain lessons in witchcraft and dangerous papist beliefs that attack our religion and the Queen herself.

WILLIAM: That is the vilest of slander! I have never practiced witchcraft nor professed any religion other than our country's own.

DOWAGER: On one occasion, when I urged him to fight against the Catholics, he refused most violently.

WILLIAM: Because it was outrageous.

DOWAGER: Outrageous to fight against Catholics? Put that in the record, too, my good scribe.

JUDGE: Will you state to the Court the content of your writings?

WILLIAM: I prefer not to do so, for personal reasons. But I swear by my honor that they have nothing whatsoever to do with these accusations.

JUDGE: It is my responsibility to oblige you to make a public statement.

WILLIAM: In that case . . . they're plays. Dramas, comedies, tragedies.

JUDGE: Plays? For the theater?

DOWAGER: Good Heavens, you can come up with a less ridiculous excuse than that.

JUDGE: Show me your writings, milord.

WILLIAM: I don't have them. You see . . . I've given them to someone.

JUDGE: To whom?

WILLIAM: To . . . an actor. So he can stage them.

DOWAGER: A nobleman mixed up with lowly vagrants and actors? What a disgrace!

WILLIAM: Actors are Her Majesty's subjects, too.

DOWAGER: Scum! That's only tolerated because their clowning amuses.

LADY DERBY: They bore me.

DOWAGER: It wouldn't be that Shakespeare fellow, or whatever his name is?

LADY DERBY: Who's that?

DOWAGER: An actor poet who's quite famous.

LADY DERBY: I've never heard of him.

DOWAGER: Just imagine, Your Honor, more than once he has said—do I dare repeat it?—that he is the author of those celebrated works!

WILLIAM: What if I told you it's true?

DOWAGER: I would respond—in the words of that Spanish novel they call the Quixote—that from so much reading and so much writing, your brains have dried up.

WILLIAM: What are you insinuating?

DOWAGER: Well, if you're not a sorcerer or a heretic but claim to be a famous playwright, then you've lost your reason, for you believe your hallucinations. There's a name for that. It's called madness.

WILLIAM: I'm a madman?

DOWAGER: Who, but a madman, would dare to usurp the identity of another in order to appropriate his glory?

LADY DERBY: Don't forget to tell how he tried to strangle me.

JUDGE: Strangle you, my good Countess?

LADY DERBY: (Putting her hands around her neck) Like this. I couldn't breathe.

DOWAGER: Fortunately, I was there to save her from this wild man's fury.

JUDGE: (To William) It that true?

WILLIAM: Because she was unfaithful to me!

DOWAGER: Another of his hallucinations!

LADY DERBY: I was always virtuous and submissive.

DOWAGER: Obviously! No one in his right mind could doubt it. Only a madman could believe this sweet creature was capable of inappropriate conduct.

WILLIAM: I have proof of her betrayal. The handkerchief!

DOWAGER: A handkerchief! Scribe, put that in the record. A tiny piece of cloth. It would be laughable if it weren't so pathetic. All ladies and gentlemen carry a handkerchief to alleviate the discharge from their nostrils. You, Your Honor, no doubt have a handkerchief in your pocket. Even the scribe . . .

LADY DERBY: I lost it in one of the drawing rooms at Court.

DOWAGER: I ask the Court, who has not at some time lost a handkerchief? So little it slips through your fingers. If everyone who had lost a handkerchief were strangled, there'd be no one left in all England.

WILLIAM: But that one was found in a gentleman's chamber!

DOWAGER: Who invented such a falsehood? Did you perchance see it? No! It was a servant! Only a madman would give credence to a common servant rather than to his irreproachable wife.

LADY DERBY: And he was so miserly that for my personal expenses he gave me a paltry thousand pounds.

WILLIAM: Because this viper deprived me of the inheritance that is rightfully mine.

DOWAGER: And why did your brother disinherit you? Because your hallucinations and your obsessions prevent you from taking care of your own estate, which has fallen into the most lamentable decay.

WILLIAM: You're defaming me for the sole purpose of gaining the sympathy of this Court.

JUDGE: You are maligning the impartiality of this Court!

WILLIAM: This Court, its impartiality, and all these documents are pure farce.
(He picks up the papers and throws them on the floor.)

JUDGE: You will answer for contempt of court!

WILLIAM: And you will answer for your complicity with the dirty tricks of these spiteful ladies!
(Costrand, as scribe, kneels to pick up the papers.)

DOWAGER: Your Honor, I believe the mental state of my good brother-in-law has become patently clear and that he constitutes a threat not only to the dignity of his noble name but also to the persons around him. I therefore petition this Court to remove from him the rights and responsibilities of his title, that you declare him incompetent to administer the county, that the administration thereof be assigned to his wife . . .

LADY DERBY: Quite so.

DOWAGER: . . . and that he be confined to his chambers so he may be properly attended, given his dangerous malady.

WILLIAM: What is this old hag saying? She wants to lock me up like a madman?

DOWAGER: Naturally, that decision will be made by the court of law.

WILLIAM: Your Honor, all this is but malicious stories spread by an adulterous wife and a spiteful woman whom I refused to marry.

DOWAGER: How dare you say such a thing! It was I who refused his outrageous proposal whose sole purpose was to recover the properties he had lost because of his dim wits.

WILLIAM: Why, you even spoke of uniting two branches to form a single trunk.

DOWAGER: In trying to convince me, he compared me to a little branch, with tender leaves. To be sure, that was the only agreeable part of his conversation.

WILLIAM: I would never have said such an insipid thing!

DOWAGER: Your Honor will understand my indignation. He was proposing marriage when my noble husband's body had scarcely been placed in the tomb.

WILLIAM: That didn't keep you from embracing me most shamelessly.

DOWAGER: Oh! If the seriousness of the moment did not prevent me from doing so, I would faint on the spot.

JUDGE: Courage, my lady.

WILLIAM: Before you succeed in your hypocritical, lying schemes, I swear I'll kill you . . . both!

JUDGE: My good lord, calm yourself.

WILLIAM: *(Beside himself)* Take that, you wicked, conniving, thieving reptile who has taken away what is mine!

DOWAGER: *(Frightened)* Don't you dare touch me! You rotten, uncouth villain!

JUDGE: *(Rising to intervene)* Be calm, my lord and lady. Calm yourselves.

WILLIAM: And you, you unfaithful bitch, you adulterous slut!

LADY DERBY: Help, he's killing me!

DOWAGER: Murderer!

(In the midst of the fight the judge gets hit from both sides.)

JUDGE: Don't hit me! I'm the judge!

WILLIAM: Witch!

DOWAGER: Rogue!

LADY DERBY: He's mad, a madman . . .

WILLIAM: Whore!

JUDGE: *(Pounding his gavel furiously on the table)* Enough, enough, enough! Order in the court. Silence!
(They fall silent. Pause)

DOWAGER: With Your Honor's permission, to avoid further angry attacks like the one we have just witnessed—and that I trust the scribe has duly recorded—we should like to withdraw.

JUDGE: *(Rising to bid them farewell)* My good ladies . . .

WILLIAM: You're going to let them leave like that, without waiting for my response?

JUDGE: My lord, you may be sure justice will make the most appropriate decision for your noble person.

DOWAGER: Before leaving this room, I should like to make a last statement. The Countess and I, as devout Christians, forgive the noble Earl for all his insults, nasty remarks, lies, and despicable deeds.

LADY DERBY: *(To the Dowager Countess)* We do?

DOWAGER: Let's be charitable. The poor fellow is . . . *(Gesturing to indicate madness)*

WILLIAM: What am I hearing? That they forgive me? Me?

DOWAGER: We shall pray every day that the Lord return him to his right mind.

LADY DERBY: We shall pray every day. Amen.

DOWAGER: Amen.

(The Countesses exit)

WILLIAM: Where are they going? I forbid you to leave! They have to listen to me!

JUDGE: I'm sorry, my lord. The court is adjourned.

(Costrand gathers up the documents and exits. The judge follows him.)

WILLIAM: Hey! You're not going to leave me with the words in my mouth? Scoundrels! But I shall restrain my anger and go find that Shakespeare so he can let the truth be known once and for all.

(He dons his earl's hat. Perhaps there is a change in lighting. We hear applause. The scene has shifted to a theater dressing room.)

Ah, how the audience applauds my works. There is no music to compare to the delightful sound of clapping. *(He acknowledges the applause like an author at the end of a performance.)* Thank you, thank you very much.

(Shakespeare enters, dressed in costume, with a wig and a beard.)

SHAKESPEARE: Fancy you here, my lord? It's the first time you've honored us with your presence in our theater.

WILLIAM: I have to talk to you.

SHAKESPEARE: Sit down. I apologize for not having a better chair to offer you.

WILLIAM: I have come to right wrongs and to unmask my defamers.

SHAKESPEARE: Sir, I don't understand.

WILLIAM: What were you performing?

SHAKESPEARE: *The Tragedy of Macbeth.*

WILLIAM: *(Reciting)* "Hail, King! For so thou art.

Behold where stands

The usurper's cursèd head."

SHAKESPEARE: *(Continuing the speech)* "The time is free.

I see thee compassed with thy kingdom's pearl,

That speak my salutation in their minds,

Whose voices I desire aloud with mine:

Hail, King of Scotland!"

WILLIAM: *(Reciting)* "Hail, King of Scotland!" *(Sitting down)* It's beautiful, very beautiful. One of my favorite plays.

SHAKESPEARE: One of mine, too.

WILLIAM: That's precisely what I want to talk to you about.

SHAKESPEARE: What are you referring to?

WILLIAM: To *The Merchant of Venice, Julius Caesar, Henry IV,* and to all the others.

SHAKESPEARE: With your permission, I'd like to clean my face and get off this stage makeup.

(Shakespeare takes off the doublet he's wearing and removes the wig and beard. Throughout the scene he removes his makeup.)

WILLIAM: We have to undo the deception.

SHAKESPEARE: What deception, sir?

WILLIAM: You know very well what I'm referring to. Circumstances have changed since that day long ago when I made you that proposition. Powerful enemies, who wish to take over my estate, have slandered me and are trying to make me appear mad.

SHAKESPEARE: That's ridiculous.

WILLIAM: I have to demonstrate to the highest courts not just my talent but my sanity.

SHAKESPEARE: No one could doubt either one. I'd respectfully testify to it myself.

WILLIAM: I'm pleased to hear that.

SHAKESPEARE: But I fail to understand why you would resort to the testimony of a man of my condition when there are those of noble birth who could affirm it.

WILLIAM: In these turbulent times, one has to prove the obvious. Therefore I instruct you to return to me what is mine. You will have to reveal the true name that is hidden behind yours.

SHAKESPEARE: You presume to usurp my name?

WILLIAM: Only to recover my own.

SHAKESPEARE: No one throughout the realm is unfamiliar with the good Earl's glorious name.

WILLIAM: Stop playing with words. I demand that you return to me everything I have given you over the years.

SHAKESPEARE: To what do you refer?

WILLIAM: The manuscripts you receive from time to time along with some pounds.

SHAKESPEARE: My lord rewarded my work with small gifts, and I always felt honored by your favor. Perhaps you are asking me to return the money?

WILLIAM: It has nothing to do with money, although God knows I could use it, but of something far more serious. You will have to declare before the judges that I spoke the truth when I affirmed that I wrote those plays.

(Shakespeare, who has finished taking off his makeup, now turns to face William.)

SHAKESPEARE: Milord has not considered well the consequences that would bring. What would happen to the good name of Derby, of which you are so proud, when they find out you devote yourself to such vulgar pursuits?

WILLIAM: To hell with my good name! Now it's a question of life or death. For the person who is not recognized as sane is as good as dead.

SHAKESPEARE: But sir, no one will take an actor's word for it. They will all believe it is an act of cowardice milord has devised to make a mock of justice.

WILLIAM: No wellborn person could think such a thing of me.

SHAKESPEARE: Not to mention that all London acclaims the quality of my works. If you try now to take advantage of my fame, not a single resident of the city can fail to think you are indeed mad.

WILLIAM: Are you prepared to confess the truth?

SHAKESPEARE: Truth, sir, has many faces.

WILLIAM: But there is only one truth.

SHAKESPEARE: Of course. And the truth is that you and I made an agreement. Do you perhaps now intend to rescind it because it is no longer convenient for you? Noblemen like you may perhaps break your word to a commoner, but the only nobility I have is my word. And I'm not going to break it.

WILLIAM: Scoundrel!

SHAKESPEARE: I faithfully fulfilled my part of the bargain. To make your writings known, as was your desire, I visited the country's most out-of-the-way places. For the sake of those writings, I suffered hunger and cold, always in fear of becoming victim to the plague that menaced us everywhere. Now fulfill your part, too, by being faithful to the agreement.

WILLIAM: Don't oblige me to use force!

SHAKESPEARE: That would only make your situation worse. And it would be an offense to your nobility, as well as to mine.
(William becomes downcast. Shakespeare crosses to the bookcase door, which he had left open.)
Mary! Come greet his lordship!

WILLIAM: Mary is with you?

MARY: *(Entering)* My lord.

SHAKESPEARE: Bring something for milord to drink.

WILLIAM: I don't want anything from you.

MARY: I am happy to see your lordship once again.
(She starts to kiss his hand.)

WILLIAM: *(Pushing her away)* Go to hell!

MARY: Forgive me, milord, if I did not say goodbye. Lady Derby made me leave in haste, with all her attendants, without letting me go to your quarters.

WILLIAM: You could have sent me a letter.

MARY: Never have I so regretted not knowing how to write. But my lord knows the great affection this humble servant has always felt for him.

WILLIAM: How did you end up with this hooligan?

MARY: William's company of actors went to perform in a village near Oxford. I escaped from the Countess's castle and went to find them. Since then I have mended costumes and cooked their meals.

WILLIAM: And warmed his bed!

MARY: Anything is better than the abuse I received from the Countess.

WILLIAM: You slut!

SHAKESPEARE: I won't let you . . .

WILLIAM: You were always flighty, sneaky, lying, and incapable of being faithful to anyone. But I loved you. And I was filled with dismay when you left my side. Get out of my sight. I don't want to see you. Be gone!
(Mary, crying, collects the makeup paraphernalia.)
May you both go to the devil!
(Mary exits.)

SHAKESPEARE: And may he keep you in his care.
(He starts to exit.)

WILLIAM: I haven't said you could leave.

SHAKESPEARE: Excuse me, sir, but it is time for our supper. It goes without saying that you are invited to join us in our humble repast.

WILLIAM: From now on you'll have to be content with your own crow feathers and not adorn yourself in someone else's plumes like a fake peacock. To satisfy your vanity, you'll have to write your own plays. And with that your deception will be patently clear.

SHAKESPEARE: They could never compare to the ones I've already made known.

WILLIAM: You've usurped honors and applause, and maybe you'll go down in history as a genius. But the fame of which you are so proud belongs solely to my words and to my characters. Not to a charlatan like you!

SHAKESPEARE: You really think that without my help they would have been acclaimed by audiences? It's possible that they would never even have reached the stage. Because you, who never budged from your magnificent table, you ignored your creatures like some superior and distant god while I, I modified scenes, corrected mistakes, cut here and added there. Perhaps you were the one who conceived them, but I cared for them as if they were my own children; I nurtured them and turned them into what they are. They have slept with me, cried through my eyes, suffered and rejoiced with me. I am our characters, I have lived them one by one, night after night, while all you did was sketch them on a piece of paper. They would have remained mere phantoms if I had not given them life. Forgive my boldness, but sometimes I think life has turned you, a great lord, and me, a humble actor, into two sides of a single coin. May I go now? By your leave, sir.
(He exits.)

WILLIAM: What could I do after such a bitter scene? The court could hand down an unjust decision that would leave me penniless and even confine me behind these walls as a madman. But I am the one who will find reason within solitude, who will deliver his own justice, a justice that accuses me of having not honored the word given to that Shakespeare.

COSTRAND: *(Entering. The scene takes place once again in the castle.)* You called, milord?

WILLIAM: Come in.

COSTRAND: You're still writing? You'll become ill, sir. You've been at it for months and months without stopping. You scarcely eat or sleep.

WILLIAM: Today I've finished at last. I'll never write again.

COSTRAND: The Lord be praised!

WILLIAM: This is going to be my last work. My last will and testament. The one in which the poet bids farewell to the theater and to the world.

COSTRAND: You're still young to be thinking like that.

WILLIAM: It's a reflection on the art of governing, on the grotesque spectacle of intrigue and betrayal in our society. Do you understand what I'm saying, Costrand?

COSTRAND: Not a word, sir.

WILLIAM: I call it *The Tempest*.

COSTRAND: I do know what that is: thunder and lightning.

WILLIAM: My life, too, has been shipwrecked in a tempest. I have been cruel and arrogant; I have humiliated good people like yourself, sheltered behind the mask of my noble birth. Of a man who proved himself more honest than I, I demanded that he break his word. I could not even appreciate Mary's tenderness and love.

COSTRAND: Don't talk like that, sir.

WILLIAM: The world is a wicked place, virtue is hard to achieve, and even happiness is surrounded always by sorrow. One has to seek a brave new world, tinted by the colors of dream. We are such stuff as dreams are made on, and our little life is rounded with a sleep.

(He is lost in thought.)

COSTRAND: Your life isn't so bad. You have a soft bed and good food, and your only work is looking out the window at beautiful fields.

WILLIAM: Costrand, my dear Costrand. You are my only friend, the only one I have left. I can confide only in you, that is, if you are generous enough to forgive me for treating you so badly. *(Handing him a manuscript)* Here. This is the greatest treasure I possess. But be careful; it's very valuable.

COSTRAND: What am I to do with it?

WILLIAM: You remember your friend William, the actor from Stratford?

COSTRAND: That lowlife who stole Mary . . . from both of us?

WILLIAM: I bid you search for him, and wherever you find him, give him this manuscript.

COSTRAND: Give it to him?

WILLIAM: I no longer care that he's conceited and swells with pride at the expense of my talent. My work must be staged. I can't bury it with me, and he is the only one who can do it.

COSTRAND: As you wish, milord.

WILLIAM: Ask him for me to make it known throughout the theaters and the cities as he has done with the rest of my plays. Ah, and if he asks you for a pound and three and ha'pence, don't pay it. Let him do it this time for free.
(Costrand exits.)

WILLIAM: *The Tempest* was performed before King James, who had succeeded to the throne upon the death of Queen Elizabeth. Although no one in the court understood its true meaning. Naturally, Shakespeare produced no more new plays. He retired to his native town and devoted himself to administering his affairs with such extreme vigor that he had his debtors jailed for owing even small sums. The last news I had of him was brought to me by Mary, whom I had not seen since that ill-fated afternoon when I surprised her at the theater.

MARY'S VOICE: Milord, milord!
(Mary charges in, followed by Costrand.)

COSTRAND: Where are you going?

MARY: To kneel at the feet of his lordship.
(She does so.)

COSTRAND: I beg your pardon, my lord, but she started to run through the halls and up the stairs, and I couldn't catch her.

WILLIAM: How dare you appear before me? I ought to throw you to the dogs.

MARY: Have mercy, sir, I have nowhere to go.

COSTRAND: *(Grabbing her to throw her out)* Stop annoying his lordship.

MARY: *(Crying)* There's no help for me except through your kindness.

WILLIAM: *(To Costrand)* Let her go. *(To Mary)* And stop sniveling.

MARY: Forgive me, milord, but I can't. William is dead.
(Costrand crosses himself.)

WILLIAM: So that imposter has died.

MARY: Only a few days ago he was buried in the church at Stratford.

WILLIAM: Enough whimpering! That rascal didn't deserve a single tear.

MARY: He was sad and ill for a long time. His wife scolded him constantly, saying that while she had to attend to all the household chores, he only wandered about the countryside. Every day we met down at the river. He was very good to me.

WILLIAM: I don't want to know anything about your affairs.

MARY: On his birthday, Ben Jonson and other friends from London came to his house to celebrate. It must have been a very lively evening. They sat by the fire telling scandalous stories, they had a contest to see who could make up the most daring epigrams, and over and over they toasted the merry England of their youth. At dawn, William felt sick. A bit later he became delirious; although the doctor tried to revive him, he never came to.

(Costrand crosses himself again.)

WILLIAM: Perhaps I am being unjust, but God knows that, even if I wanted to, I could never forgive him for the suffering he caused me. Costrand! Open the kitchens and the wine cellars to the servants so they can rejoice with me. Let there be music and dancing!

COSTRAND: *(Sorrowfully)* But milord . . .

WILLIAM: And if you still want to marry this strumpet, you may. I give you my permission.

MARY: I don't want to marry anyone, and least of all a waif like him.

WILLIAM: *(Turning on the tape recorder to play happy music)* And now, let's dance! Everyone dance!
(Costrand and Mary hesitate.)
This is an order!
(Costrand and Mary dance without enthusiasm, taking a few reluctant steps. William immediately stops the music. To Mary)
Did he sometimes speak of me?

MARY: Frequently, sir, and always with the greatest respect.

WILLIAM: Did he give you some message? Perhaps a written note?

MARY: Why do you ask me such a question? Are you perchance clairvoyant?

WILLIAM: So he did?

MARY: One afternoon he gave me a paper, begging me to see that it reached you should he die before you.

WILLIAM: Give it to me.

MARY: I can't, sir. A few days later he asked that I return it, and he tore it up and threw the pieces in the river.

WILLIAM: Do you know what the note said?

MARY: He never told me, and I never asked.

WILLIAM: Not even posthumously was he capable of renouncing his vanity. Maybe it's better that way. It's late now, very late, far too late. Go away!
(Mary and Costrand leave.)
I must confess that, despite the hatred I felt for him, the news of his death moved me deeply. I felt as if something of myself had died, as if half of my life had been torn away from me. Perhaps he was right when he said he and I were but two sides of the same coin. But when his bones and mine are nothing but dust and a mantle of silence has sealed our lips, the creatures I conceived, my characters, will lift their voices to repeat my lines over and over on the world's stages. And they will be my verses. Mine! The ones I composed—that shall reign forever. Dear Lord, in this deceptive world does there exist anything so sublime and so banal as glory?
(Change of lighting)
And here, ladies and gentlemen, we end our tour of the castle. On your way out you will find postcards and souvenirs on sale in the coffee shop. At one time you could also have purchased a copy of the book I have just commented on for you, but it is out of print and has not been reedited. . . . It was banned.
(William closes the shutters and the stage falls into shadow, illuminated only by the light from the doorway. As he glances around the room a final time, he picks up the

skull and looks at it, half philosophically and half mockingly, then places it back on the desk. He exits through the door, closing it behind him. The stage remains in darkness except for a single ray of light that shines on the skull. The other cast members enter and, joining William, dance to happy music.)